Secrets of the Turkey Pros

Hunting Wisdom Library™

MINNETONKA, MINNESOTA

About the Author

Glenn Sapir is an outdoor communicator and has served on the editorial staffs of several outdoor magazines, including *Field & Stream*, *Outdoor Life*, *Sports Afield* and *New York Sportsman*. In addition, he contributes articles on outdoor recreation to a number of magazines, including *North American Hunter* and *North American Fisherman*. Having hunted with many of the experts in this book, he has witnessed their talents firsthand. He knows the others included in this volume by the tremendous reputations they have carved.

SECRETS OF THE TURKEY PROS

Mike Vail
Vice President, Product and Business Development

Tom Carpenter
Director of Book Development

Dan Kennedy
Book Production Manager, Photo Editor

Heather Koshiol
Book Development Coordinator

Beowulf
Book Design and Production

David Rottinghaus
Color Illustrations

Phil Aarrestad
Commissioned Photography

Recipes copyright © Sylvia Bashline.
Reprinted with permission.

PHOTO CREDITS

Sylvia Bashline: 158; Jim Casada: 110, 128, 140 (top), 142; Soc Clay: 17 (top), 20 (top), 37 (bottom), 45 (lower right), 55 (top), 56, 66 (bottom), 68, 70, 76, 77, 83 (top), 84 (top), 104, 105 (bottom), 106 (bottom), 133 (bottom), 135, 136, 138 (bottom), 162–163; Judd Cooney: 1, 18 (bottom), 19 (top), 22, 37 (top), 38, 54 (bottom), 60, 62, 64, 66 (top), 81, 87, 101, 109, 112, 122 (top), 125, 132, 134, 142 (two), 148–149, 152, 168; Michael Faw: 8–9, 18 (top), 45; Betty Lou Fegely: 16 (bottom), 46, 57, 79, 80, 154; Tom Fegely: 17 (bottom), 41, 44 (top), 52 (top), 53, 54 (top), 133 (top), 141, 142; George Harrison: 30, 31 (two); Brad Herndon: 6–7, 48–49, 78, 84, 115; Bill Hollister: 14, 71 (all), 83 (bottom), 94, 106 (top), 116, 137 (bottom), 137 (middle), 138 (top); Donald M. Jones: 13 (screen-back), 15, 23, 20 (bottom), 28, 32–33, 36, 39, 40, 42, 43 (screen-back), 44 (bottom), 45 (top left), 45 (top right), 59 (bottom), 59 (top), 63 (bottom), 63 (top), 85 (bottom), 90 (top), 93, 102–103, 107, 120, 123, 129, 140 (bottom), 151 (top), 167, 170; Mark Kayser: cover onlay, 19 (bottom), 47, 61 (bottom), 74, 88, 117, 169; Lance Krueger: 21 (five); courtesy of Mossy Oak: 73, 99; courtesy of Muzzle Blasts: 67; courtesy of National Wild Turkey Federation: 13 (left); Leonard Rue: 4, 24, 27, 34, 91, 92, 121, 164; Glenn Sapir: 2, 35, 41, 65, 69, 155; Keith Sutton: 12; courtesy of Wildlife Forever: 13 (right); Lovett Williams: 26, 29. Remaining photographs property of NAOG: 16 (top), 50, 52 (bottom), 55 (bottom), 61 (top), 72, 75, 82, 84 (bottom), 85 (top), 86, 89, 90 (bottom), 94, 97, 108, 144, 150, 156.

8 7 6 5 4 3 / 03 02 01 00

ISBN 1-58159-038-5

North American Hunting Club
12301 Whitewater Drive
Minnetonka, MN 55343
www.huntingclub.com

Table of Contents

ACKNOWLEDGEMENTS: I have to thank many people for the creation of this book. Most importantly are the experts whose words you will read, and the photographers and artists whose images you'll enjoy. The North American Outdoor Group book department's staff of Tom Carpenter, Heather Koshiol and Dan Kennedy supervised the project with professionalism and a gentle demeanor. Nancy Concia of Intelligent Solutions, Croton-on-Hudson, NY, facilitated my work by transcribing the interviews with the experts. Many members of the National Wild Turkey Federation graciously lent assistance. Charlie Gardner, John Miller and the late Bob Wright took me to the poult stage of turkey hunting. Bill Hollister has made me at least a jake. Many of the other experts in this book have shared their time and knowledge afield with me. Sherry Makela and Ed Rylee of the Outdoor Alliance Group have given me the opportunity to grow even more as a turkey hunter. My wife Nancy and my children have tolerated my predawn departures and frequent out-of-town hunts and have always given me their unwavering support and love. To all I give my heartfelt thanks.

—Glenn Sapir

Foreword

North American Hunting Club members who hunt wild turkey are generally split between two philosophies about why the birds can be so hard to bag. One says that the turkey is so smart, possesses such incredible hearing and eyesight, and is so spooky that we are simply lucky ever to kill one. The second philosophy says that we are dealing with a bird that has a brain so small and that is so inherently fickle, we are left trying to outguess a critter that doesn't even know itself what it's going to do from one second to the next!

What both sides of the debate have in common is respect for the turkey as a wily, challenging game animal. In fact, it can be said that the turkey is the big game of small game or the small game of big game animals—another interesting debate for hunting camp.

Regardless of which turkey subspecies you hunt or where you hunt them, pursuing gobblers has one more thing in common: Hunting them is about as exciting as hunting gets.

You'll often hear spring turkey hunting called "poor man's elk hunting." While it holds similarities to calling elk during the rut, this comparison doesn't give the turkey its full due. Turkey can be hunted in 49 states. In most cases the seasons are longer, and in many places the limit allows you to take more than one turkey per year. You can purchase licenses over the counter in most places. Hunting grounds are easier to find and easier to access. Success in bagging a bird is far more likely for the self-guided hunter than for the unguided elk hunter. In other words—turkeys offer similar excitement to hunting bugling elk, to a lot more hunters. Perhaps that's the turkey's greatest gift to us all!

In the pages of this exclusive North American Hunting Club edition you'll come to cherish that gift, experience that excitement—in the spring or fall—and learn how to get in on the game yourself. Hopefully you'll pick up a few hints to help you outwit those "super-smart" birds or out-guess those "super-fickle" ones—depending which side of the fence you sit on.

Take care and good turkey hunting!

Best afield,

Bill

Bill Miller
Executive Director, North American Hunting Club

INTRODUCTION

*I*f you are a novice turkey hunter, then anyone who can put a diaphragm call in his or her mouth and make sounds come out might seem like an expert to you. If you are an experienced turkey hunter who's made his share of mistakes to go along with the successes, then you are probably a lot more discerning about who the real experts are. If you are considered an expert—or a pro, as the title of this book suggests—you know how inappropriate the title really is.

That's because all too often the true expert in turkey hunting is the gobbler that gets away: the one that teases you with his thundering responses but never struts within shooting range; the one that sneaks in on you silently while you move your hands to strike a slate call for a bird you mistakenly thought would come from the opposite direction; the one that is actually two, the second spotting you as you slowly position your gun to aim at the first, his alarm putts ending all hope of a victory.

Yet if turkeys could talk in human words, they would acknowledge that they have been up against a few experts. Several of those people have been recruited to "talk turkey" with us on the pages that follow.

You've heard of some of these experts, maybe even seen them on television or at a seminar. But you almost certainly have no prior knowledge of others. Those few neither write articles nor have many articles written about them in the sporting magazines—they simply know more than most about a particular aspect of the bird or the sport. They are all excellent hunters, yet the credentials that landed them on these pages have far more to do with the knowledge they have accumulated than their ability to emit a fly-down cackle or emulate a kee-kee run.

It is their words that you will read, enjoy, sometimes chuckle at and certainly profit from. They will explore the world of the wild turkey and the sport in which we participate. They will teach you enough, no matter how much or little you currently know, to get even closer to becoming an expert—the kind that even a wild gobbler would be proud to talk to.

—Glenn Sapir

Chapter 1

UNDERSTANDING THE WILD TURKEY

When a hunter steps into the wild turkey's world, he is becoming part of a glorious story. Though many people know of the wild turkey's great comeback, few know how low turkey numbers really dropped or how the birds have returned to ancestral ranges that were perhaps void for a century or more.

Other hunters wonder at the presence of a magnificent game bird in areas where recorded history makes no mention of turkeys ever having been there before. Few know that the supermarket turkey can trace its roots to a North American wild bird that was domesticated in Europe and then reintroduced to this continent.

A hunter may know that a wild tom turkey might gobble to an artificial hen yelp on a spring day, but that same hunter may know relatively little of how the birds communicate in general. Though he spends much time in the laboratory of the outdoors during the turkey hunting seasons, how much does the hunter truly know of the wild turkey's day-to-day activities, much less the bird's survival tactics during the rest of the year?

The pros we've enlisted here *know* turkeys. Mary and Dr. James Earl Kennamer have spent years researching and writing about the wild turkey. They can trace the history of the wild turkey from prehistoric times to today. They know the life cycle of the wild turkey, from the time the egg is laid until the day the adult—if that embryo in the egg is lucky enough to become an adult—meets its end.

They know the subtle variations between the five subspecies of wild turkeys in the Americas, and the far more different characteristics of an exotic species found in southern Mexico and Central America.

Join the Kennamers as they take you through the world of the wild turkey—past and present, near and not-so-near.

A History of America's wild Turkey

*T*he wild turkey we hunt today carries a fascinating history. Like the Roman Empire, our wild turkey has experienced its own rise and fall. Fortunately for the species—and for hunters—turkeys have once again experienced a rise. Rather than taking for granted the birds' wide availability, we as hunters would be wise to familiarize ourselves with the wild turkey's history to truly appreciate what we have today and how fortunate we are.

A North American Original

The wild turkey is a North American native. Fossils of now-extinct species and subspecies inhabiting the pre-Columbus continent have been found. It is believed that American Indians domesticated two subspecies of wild turkey; today's Merriam's subspecies is possibly a feral form of the larger of the two.

Humans began domesticating turkeys by gathering eggs from wild birds in Mexico. By 1520, Spanish conquistadors had brought some of these domesticated turkeys back to Spain, where the birds were then introduced to other parts of Europe. So the domestic strain of turkey that we know today evolved from a once wild, now believed extinct, turkey of Mexico. Strangely enough, it was European settlers who introduced this domesticated bird to the New World; it was brought to Jamestown, Virginia, around 1607 and to Massachusetts in 1629. Quite a homecoming.

In the meantime, American Indians were capturing wild turkeys with nets, snares and pens. The birds were unwary and easily taken, so much so that they were not considered worthy game for most experienced hunters. Though some tribes did not consider wild turkey a delicacy, it was a significant source of food for many others. In addition, the feathers were used in clothing. Awls and spoons were made from turkey bones. Of course, many arrows utilized turkey feathers as fletching, and some tribes used leg spurs as arrow tips. Feathers were also used for masks and head-

"Planter Rendezvous—Eastern Wild Turkeys" by Jim Kasper. Courtesy of the artist and Wild Wings Inc., Lake City, MN 55041. 1-800-445-4833.

dresses; feathers and bristles from beards were placed on prayer sticks; and legs were sometimes hung from pierced ears.

At the time Europeans arrived and began settling the east coast, it is believed that wild turkeys ranged through at least the territory that now makes up 39 states and Ontario.

Turkey Fallacies ... and the Turkey's Fall

Despite popular belief, turkey was neither the main course of the first Thanksgiving meal nor the bird championed for our national seal by Benjamin Franklin. Turkey more likely became a Thanksgiving staple at the end of the 18th century. The committee deciding on a national symbol (made up of Thomas Jefferson, John Adams and Benjamin Franklin in 1776) could not come up with a clear choice, though no one supported the wild turkey. However, Franklin wrote (in a private letter to his daughter in 1784) about the negative aspects of the bald eagle and the admirable traits of the wild turkey—but that occurred long after the symbol of the eagle had been selected.

About the Expert

Dr. James Earl Kennamer is vice president for conservation programs with the National Wild Turkey Federation. He writes "Biologically Speaking," a regular feature in *Turkey Call* magazine, and has also authored more than 50 scientific papers, including chapters in four books.

Dr. Kennamer received the C. W. Watson Award, the highest honor bestowed by the Southeastern Association of Fish and Wildlife Agencies, Southern Division of the American Fisheries Society and Southeastern Section of the Wildlife Society, for distinguished service in wildlife research and administration.

Too many good hunts like this—for the market and for the home larder—contributed to the wild turkey's decline. Large-scale clearing of forests hurt just as much.

Great flocks of wild turkeys were reported in various settlements. For example, the Dutch settlers of New Netherland, which later became New York state, reported innumerable turkeys. Flocks of 500 were reported in North Carolina in 1709. Lewis and Clark reported sightings in several states, noting that they observed "... turkeys in great quantities on the bank." Bartram wrote in Florida of being awakened by "turkey-cocks saluting each other" from treetops.

Wild turkeys proved an important food source for the settlers, so it is no wonder that turkeys quickly began to disappear with unregulated, year-round hunting. The rapid clearing of forests—as well as the pressure of market hunting to feed the new country's growing towns—also contributed to the wild turkey's demise. Turkeys were extirpated from Connecticut by 1813. By 1920, the birds were gone from 18 of the original 39 states that supported wild turkey populations, as well as Ontario. In the remaining states, only the most inaccessible and isolated regions continued to hold birds.

LOW EBB, NEW BEGINNINGS

The lowest ebb of the national wild turkey population was probably in the late 1930s. But the days of the Great Depression and the Dust Bowl era, which drove many tenant and land-owning farmers off their property, set the stage for a dramatic reversal in the fortunes of the wild turkey. Conservation practices (including restricted hunting seasons or none at all) and new laws (such as the one that banned the interstate sale of harvested wildlife) helped pave the way for a comeback. This happened in tandem with the land's recovery as it reverted to forest.

To add to the good situation, the Pittman-Robertson Act of 1937 brought revenue to state wildlife recovery attempts through its excise tax on sporting goods and ammunition. This made funding for restoration efforts possible: The wild turkey could be restocked in the recovering habitat. But the technology to carry out this restoration was lagging. The trapping and transfer of wild turkeys to new, inhabitable areas is the backbone of recent restoration efforts, but the technology of the 1940s and '50s had not yet produced an effective means of trapping the birds.

Instead, states tried to take the only quick way to start populations—by artificially propagating birds, using eggs taken from wild turkey nests or from captured hen turkeys. This proved to be a

Some Important Milestones in Modern Wild Turkey Restoration

1905   Lacey Act prohibits the interstate sale of taken wildlife, affording some protection to existing wild turkeys.

1920   Wild turkeys extirpated from 18 states of their original 39-state range and their ancestral home.

1930s Wild turkeys in the United States reach their lowest numbers. Abandoned farms and other previously harvested forest areas begin reverting to successional shrubs and trees.

1933   Wildlife management movement gains credibility with the publication of Aldo Leopold's book of game management principles.

1937   The Pittman-Robertson Act passes, providing funds to initiate wildlife recovery programs.

1940s State wildlife departments undertake programs of raising "wild" birds in captivity and releasing them. This concept proves ineffective and costly, setting back successful turkey restoration.

1943   Henry S. Mosby and Charles Handley publish *The Wild Turkey in Virginia*, ushering in a new era of research and management.

1951   First successful turkey live trapping occurs, using a cannon net.

1959   First National Wild Turkey Symposium takes place. Wild turkey populations estimated at 500,000 in the U.S.

1970   Wild turkey populations estimated at 600,000 in the U.S. Second National Wild Turkey Symposium is held. (Since then, symposia have been staged every five years.)

1973   The National Wild Turkey Federation (NWTF) is founded.

1975   U.S. wild turkey populations estimated at 1,300,000.

1980   U.S. wild turkey populations estimated at 1,750,000.

1986   U.S. wild turkey populations estimated at 2,600,000.

1990   U.S. wild turkey populations estimated at 3,360,000.

Present U.S. wild turkey populations estimated at 4 million.

A cannon net capturing wild turkeys.

Releasing a wild turkey into new habitat.

financial debacle and biological failure, for it was discovered that birds deprived of normal rearing in the wild could not develop necessary skills to survive once released to the wild.

The advent of the cannon net, originally designed to capture waterfowl, opened the door to widespread trapping of wild turkeys. The technique involves concealing a net that is propelled by electrically detonated cannons or rocket projectiles. A person concealed in a nearby blind controls the device. It was first used on turkeys in South Carolina in 1951.

Then things began to snowball.

A Full-Fledged Comeback

According to Dr. Kennamer, "The restoration of the wild turkey kind of came along in the '60s, slowly gaining momentum, and of course in the last 20 years has just done phenomenally with increasing the number of birds. We may have 4.2 million wild turkeys in the country today. They are hunted in every state except Alaska, and inhabit most of the Canadian border provinces."

Dr. Kennamer's own organization, the National Wild Turkey Federation (NWTF), is an important part of the history of the wild turkey. "We started in 1973, founded in Fredericksburg, Virginia, by Tom Rodgers, who very quickly moved it to Edgefield, South Carolina. From an organization that at first simply ran calling contests, it developed a mission dedicated to the conservation of the wild turkey and then added to that mission the preservation of the turkey-hunting tradition."

From creating transport boxes for turkeys in transit—"We've given out more than 100,000 of them"—to funding a significant part of some states' turkey programs, the National Wild Turkey Federation has played a key role in the wild turkey's comeback.

"With our sponsors and our many partners, we

You can now see large flocks of wild turkeys in areas where wild turkeys may have been rare or nonexistent only a few decades ago. Such a sight symbolizes a tremendous wildlife management success.

have generated more than $90 million for the wild turkey over the years," Dr. Kennamer continues. "At a recent National Wild Turkey Symposium that we co-sponsored with other partners, of the projects reported that were peer reviewed, 92 percent were sponsored either in part or in their entirety by the NWTF."

All these combined efforts led to what Dr. Kennamer refers to as one of the conservation marvels of this century. "We came from 30,000 birds at the lowest point of the 1900s to over 4 million today," he declares.

The comeback of the wild turkey is a great story, perhaps the century's most incredible conservation accomplishment. So the next time you're out in the spring woods and hear that thunderous gobble, take a few seconds to appreciate the experience! Without the dedicated effort of yesterday's and today's sportsmen, you wouldn't be hearing that wonderful sound and listening to your heart pound as you plan your hunting setup.

Author's Note:

Dr. Kennamer, who has also been director of research and management for the National Wild Turkey Federation, collaborated with Mary Kennamer (formerly the information specialist for that same department of the federation) and Ron Brenneman (also a former staff member of that department) to research the bird's history diligently for a chapter in The Wild Turkey: Biology & Management, *which was edited by James G. Dickson and published by Stackpole Books. The entire book is a treasure trove of information on the wild turkey.*

Dr. Kennamer shares his and his colleagues' knowledge through "National Wild Turkey Federation Wildlife Bulletins" and a lengthy conversation with me. It is a privilege to be able to impart this information, provided by such an illustrious source, to the readers of this book.

PROFILING THE WILD TURKEY

*I*f you think of a domesticated turkey when the word "turkey" is mentioned, then you are thinking of a different bird in most respects. "The wild turkey is much leaner," explains Dr. James Earl Kennamer. "The legs are much stouter because the wild bird has to run to get away from danger. In contrast, the domestic turkey has been bred for the big breast and big legs, and a problem it has is actually being able to support itself. While the domestic bird may reach 40 pounds, a big wild

The "beard"—a bristly protrusion from the chest—is actually a modified feather. Some gobblers have multiple beards. Bearded hens are uncommon.

turkey gobbler weighs around 20 pounds. In the Midwest cornbelt, you might get them up to 25, even 30 pounds, with all that good grain to eat."

Wild turkey hens are smaller and lighter in coloration. "The hens weigh around 8 or 10 pounds. Their coloration is a buff and light brown, which allows them to blend into vegetation better than the gobbler—an advantage during the nesting season. The gobbler appears black, more iridescent."

Kennamer adds, "The wild turkey has to run and fly, so it has very good musculature, not the fat you would find on the domestic bird—except for the breast sponge during the spring."

A Unique Bird

Hunters put great stock in two features of the gobbler's body: the beard, a bristly protrusion from the chest; and the spurs, sharp attachments to the legs. "We don't know the function of the beard, which really is a modified feather. The spurs are obviously for fighting. There is very little fighting to the death among turkeys; the fighting between gobblers usually ends when one realizes he is not going to be the dominant bird," says Kennamer.

Body and wing feathers act as both waterproofing and insulation. Hunters who make the mistake of taking futile body shots at a turkey, rather than at the more vulnerable head and neck area, realize that the cold is not the only thing from which the thick feathers insulate a gobbler.

A turkey's acute senses of sight and hearing also insulate it from danger. Hunters are continually amazed at the bird's ability to home in on calls and to pick up even the slightest movement (like when you shift your gun to aim and take a shot). Their sense of smell, on the other hand, is very poor.

A Turkey's Day

Turkeys will generally roost in trees overnight, and as soon as they fly down at first light they begin scratching and feeding. "If they are with a flock, they are like a moving unit, feeding until late afternoon. They might loaf during the middle of the day, hanging out in the shade in very hot weather," Kennamer describes. "In general, however, they feed all day."

To say that their diet is varied would be an understatement. "We've got a record of over 400 different things that wild turkeys eat," says Kennamer. "Winter foods are primarily mast—acorns, beechnuts and foods like that. Turkeys feed on dogwood, hawthorn and most any other berry. They eat fruits, like wild grapes. They like seeds from grasses and legumes. Clover and alfalfa are on the menu too—turkeys are opportunistic."

In agricultural country, farmers know only too well the turkey's penchant for grain, especially corn and wheat. Turkeys are not especially destructive to mature crops, but they can ravage a field of new corn whose ears are just sprouting, or

The spurs on a gobbler's legs are an aid in fighting. A turkey's spurs and beard serve as trophies for hunters.

Mast, such as acorns and beechnuts, are favorite foods. But turkeys are opportunistic feeders; biologists have identified more than 400 foods that turkeys rely on.

destroy the succulent sprouts in a winter wheat field if there isn't much snow cover. In farm country, turkeys will even follow cows around in winter, picking whole grain out of the patties the cows leave behind.

"Turkeys feed heavily on insects when available—grasshoppers, crickets, literally any kind of insect they can pick up." Kennamer marvels, "I once shot a wild turkey that had more than 110 cicadas in its crop—and it was only 8 a.m.!"

At day's end, the birds go to roost. The predictability of where the birds will roost varies from subspecies to subspecies, of which there are five in the United States. According to Kennamer, "Eastern and Florida wild turkeys have a multitude of choices—softwoods and hardwoods—to choose from as roosting sites, so they may roost here today, then maybe half a mile away tomorrow. Merriam's and the Rio Grande turkeys are more specific, going to traditional roosting sites. Rio Grandes in particular will return to a favored roosting area, maybe a cottonwood along a stream, though the birds may fan out for several

miles during the day to feed. The Merriam's, in some of the higher elevations in particular, will roost in ponderosa pines on the south side of a slope; this offers them protection from the elements. They traditionally go to several different roost sites and may use one for two or three days, then move several miles to the next. Gould's turkeys are similar to the Rios and Merriam's in that they go to specific roosting sites, often ponderosa or Chihuahua pines."

A Turkey's Year

Of course, the birds eat during daylight and sleep during the dark hours every day, but how does their activity vary on a daily basis as the year progresses? "Let's start in late February or early March," begins Dr. Kennamer. "The birds have been flocked up for the winter. Generally, the hens will be together, the old gobblers will be together and the jakes will generally be together too. These are the three flocks you might find, though it is not unusual to find a gobbler mixed in with the hens, for instance."

Breeding
With daily sunlight lengthening in late winter and early spring, the pituitary glands produce

Turkeys roost from dusk until early morning, choosing a tree or elevated structure that will vary with the habitat.

Spring's lengthening sunlight sets off the breeding cycle, during which a dominant gobbler (background) will mate with receptive hens. This mating instinct sets the stage for spring gobbler seasons, when hunters may use hen calls to lure toms into range.

hormones in both gobblers and hens to commence the breeding cycle. The hen flocks and the gobbler flocks will break up, but the jakes will generally stay together. In some cases, jakes may join up with one or two old gobblers, but they are simply subordinates traveling with the big toms.

"As the breeding season progresses," says Kennamer, "the gobblers and hens will mate, and then, on a regular basis, the hens will leave to go to the nest. They'll lay an egg, then they may come back and get with a gobbler again during the day and stay with him until later in the nesting cycle."

"The gobblers establish a pecking order—alpha gobbler, beta gobbler, etc.—a hierarchy created through fighting. The dominant gobblers do the breeding. The subordinates get to breed only if they're by themselves and can get a hen away and on her own."

This breeding season is the center of the turkey hunter's year, the time when all is right with the world: The gobblers are talking and they're somewhat vulnerable. It's the time we all live for and hunting this season effectively is the subject of much of this book.

"Then, as the season progresses in the spring—

April and May—the hens will lay about 12 eggs, 1 per day, and they'll incubate the eggs over a 28-day period, sitting on the nest to keep it warm and to protect it from small predators. She'll leave the nest for only short periods to feed."

Raising the Young

"Once the eggs start to hatch, it takes about a day for them all to open. The new brood and hen then become kind of a moving unit. She takes them into brood habitat, where there is fairly low vegetation and good overhead cover. Her best defense from predators for these young poults is being concealed. If there is a danger, she will

A hen will lay an egg a day until she has a clutch of about a dozen. The eggs require 28 days of incubation.

A hen's brood is vulnerable to ground and aerial predators, so she will keep them in low vegetation with overhead cover.

make an alarm putt, and the poults will freeze. You could crawl around on your hands and knees trying to feel for them, and they would not move. At this time, until they are about six weeks old, they are most vulnerable."

"When they are about two weeks old, the young turkeys can fly," Dr. Kennamer continues. "As soon as they can, they will fly up at night to some low vegetation to roost, to avoid predators. A young turkey's most vulnerable time in its first six weeks is when it is rained on or if the weather is cold and damp for three or four days. In a rainstorm, the hen will try to keep her poults dry and warm by making an umbrella with her wings. In any case, about 50 percent of the eggs laid don't result in turkeys that live beyond their first several weeks, whether it is weather, predators, logging, farming or other perils that befall them."

"During those summer months, the hen will keep the brood with her. In fact, they will stay together until the fall, when they split up into their separate flocks consisting of hens and jakes."

The Gobbler's Role

How do the gobblers spend their days? "During the spring, turkeys are basically breeding machines," explains Dr. Kennamer. "They have been feeding during the winter, developing what's called a breast sponge on their chest. That is a

The hen will keep her brood with her through the summer until the fall breakup, when the birds split up into flocks of juvenile toms (jakes) and a combination of juvenile (jennies) and adult hens. A poult's most vulnerable time is during its first six weeks.

Understanding the Wild Turkey

Once the gobbling instinct takes hold, a dominant tom will be totally consumed with breeding. He will frequently gobble (above) to attract hens. With his gobble, he invites hens to come to him—the opposite of what hunters attempt to do in calling in toms.

layer of fatty tissue that is usually three or four pounds in weight. That tissue helps sustain them during the exhaustive breeding season. So, early in the spring, a gobbler will have a big breast because he hasn't absorbed much of that fat yet." But that fat will soon start to be absorbed because instead of feeding, the gobbler will be concentrating all his time, energy, attention and effort on breeding.

"They are displaying," Dr. Kennamer points out. "They're gobbling to attract hens. In fact, when you hunt, you are trying to get the tom to come to you, making him do the opposite of what nature has programmed him to do. He'll stand out in an opening and gobble and strut. The hens will come to him. When a hen is ready to mate, she goes into what is called a sexual crouch. The hen will lie down on the ground, inviting the gobbler to climb up on her back and breed. Once they finish breeding, which takes from 2 to 10 minutes, the

Merriam's hen and gobbler breeding.

Turkey Fight!

Text and photos by Lance Krueger

Scraping the chalked-up paddle of my box call to mimic an excited hen turkey, my sequence was cut short by an approaching gobbler somewhere in front of us. Two friends, having never seen nor heard a wild turkey, sat on each side of me totally covered in borrowed camouflage to blend in with the South Texas brush. Even my weapon of choice that morning, a Canon camera and 300mm telephoto lens, was covered with camouflage. Just when I felt the Rio Grande gobbler was about to step into the opening in front of us, I unexpectedly heard the "spit-drum" of a different gobbler going to full strut at close range to our left. Slowly moving my head toward the sound, I saw a different gobbler at full-strut with a subordinate jake at 15 yards. Earlier, we heard him gobble once far behind us, but he seemed less excited than the bird to our front. This pair had beaten the excited gobbler in a footrace by only seconds.

Making his entrance at the edge of the brush, the excited gobbler turned from lover to fighter when he saw he had lost the race. The longbeards immediately walked toward each other with an unmistakable, aggressive demeanor. A crescendo of aggressive purring and gobbling began as the birds approached each other. They bumped chests at 40 yards from our ringside seat. Circling with their left wings nearly touching as challenging gladiators once did, the equally matched rivals tried to show who was bigger and tougher.

I started firing my camera at them as they began to flail each other with their wings and peck at each other's heads. A couple dozen times they jumped simultaneously into the air and beat each other with their wings, each stabbing his enemy with his 1¹/₂-inch-long spurs. When they landed back on earth, the combatants would push each other with their chests in a shoving match as they vied for position. After three minutes of pummeling each other, the silent gobbler retreated in defeat with the jake. The excited gobbler had won, and he chased and gobbled after the interlopers, seeming to forget about his prize. Like flies on a wall, we had witnessed some spectacular yet seldom-seen turkey behavior.

Seeing the gobblers departing from the stage before us, I came up with an idea. I whispered to the shaking, camouflaged blob on my right to take off his baseball cap, and to whack it intermittently against his knee to sound like the fighting birds' wings hitting each other. Quickly pulling out my Knight & Hale Fighting Purr calls, I imitated the alternating, aggressive purring we had just heard. Seconds after starting our mock-fight, the victorious gobbler was running straight toward us with wings down and feathers bristled in an aggressive posture. He nearly ran right over us in our shaking boots! All of us thought the bruiser was going to flail us, just like he had done to his vanquished foe. Momentarily, the tom zigzagged in front of us too close for my telephoto lens to focus but long enough to leave an image that will replay in my mind for the rest of my life.

Understanding the Wild Turkey

gobbler preens his feathers, shakes his feathers and goes back to strutting for another hen. He's constantly doing this throughout the breeding season."

"One hen may mate with several different gobblers. A hen stores the sperm in her oviduct, where it can last for about 30 days. So, one mating by a hen is literally sufficient for her to be able to complete a clutch of eggs. As the yolk comes down the reproductive tract, the sperm fertilizes it. When an egg travels down the next day, the same thing happens. As alluded to, several gobblers will usually mate with a hen; so when the hen lays her eggs, poults in one clutch may have a variety of fathers."

"As the breeding season winds down, the hen sits on the nest and then raises the brood. The nest she creates usually is in low, thick vegetation and as hidden as she possibly can make it. The gobbler becomes a lot more mobile at this time.

He'll travel more and continue to gobble. The poor guy is still trying to find hens, but they will be preoccupied with their incubation duties. It is at this time that the breeding shuts down. The tom will get back together with some of the other gobblers, and they will spend their summer together. The hens, of course, will stay with their poults during the summer."

Autumn & Winter

By early autumn, each flock has established its own pecking order. The young have developed survival skills, and both parental and breeding behavior probably will not again become apparent until the next spring. The birds may move to a new habitat to find appropriate food or cover. In the summer they were primarily in fields, meadows and other open areas; in the fall, they will shift more to forests and feed on the available food there, including mast such as acorns. This is

Winter flocks of turkeys range as mobile units, feeding and scratching. They'll dig through the snow to find food. At least one of the flock is usually looking up, serving as a sentinel alert to danger.

Turkeys will travel in the winter months. These Merriam's turkeys might migrate 40 miles to winter range. By the end of winter, as days get longer, hormones trigger the mating instinct, and the entire breeding cycle begins again.

in contrast to the insects and vegetation that sustain them during the spring and summer. The insects, high in protein, are nutritionally important to the rapidly growing poults.

Birds do not typically settle into a winter range until snow accumulates or cold weather really takes hold, usually after the fall hunting seasons are over. Then turkeys may concentrate into relatively large flocks. Eastern birds may roost on slopes that offer protection and a view, probably even some sunlight to warm up, much like the spots deer choose to bed. In fact, turkeys in winter have often been spotted roosting directly over bedded deer. Hemlocks provide optimum protection as roost sites during snowstorms.

"The three different flocks—gobblers, subadult gobblers (jakes) and the hens—range as mobile units," Dr. Kennamer describes. "As the turkeys move in flocks of perhaps a dozen birds, they feed and scratch, that is, turn over leaves and dig into the soil to find food. Generally, at least one of them is looking up, serving as a sentinel alert to danger. If a predator scatters the flock, the turkeys will call each other to come back

together; they may even roost in the same area of trees that night."

"During the winter months turkeys are going to travel. How far depends on the amount of food that is available. Merriam's turkeys in the West may inhabit high elevations—to 9,000 feet—in the summer and fall. Their movement from summer to winter range may be 30 to 40 miles! They come down as the snow and cold weather push them into lower elevations."

In the South and Midwest, turkeys will home in to areas of good mast production in the forests, as well as agricultural fields that may offer grain to glean. The farther north one gets, too much snow can be a problem for turkeys because it covers their food sources deeper than the birds can scratch down to.

"By the end of winter, as days get longer, hormones trigger the breeding instinct, and the cycle begins again," Kennamer concludes. This is also the time of high anticipation for the turkey hunter, waiting for and preparing for the upcoming hunting season.

Understanding the Wild Turkey

THE FIVE NORTH AMERICAN SUBSPIECES

—∿— EASTERN —∿—

(Meleagris gallopavo silvestris)

The Eastern wild turkey is the most widely distributed, abundant and hunted of the five distinct subspecies found in the United States. It inhabits roughly the eastern half of the country and has been successfully introduced to three northwestern states: California, Oregon and Washington. You will find Easterns in hardwood and mixed forests from New England and southern Canada to northern Florida and west to Texas, Missouri, Iowa and Minnesota. Its habitat can range from wilderness to suburbs.

Eastern turkeys tend to grow larger than any of the other subspecies. The adult male, called a gobbler or tom, can stand as tall as four feet and weigh more than 20 pounds. His upper tail coverts, which cover the base of the long tail feathers, are tipped with chestnut brown and his tail tips with dark buff or chocolate brown. The breast feathers are tipped in black. Other body feathers show a metallic, copper or bronze iridescence.

The primary wing feathers have white and black bars that run from their edge to the shaft. Secondary wing feathers have prominent white bars and are edged in white, producing a whitish triangle on each side of the back when the wings are folded on the back.

The mature Eastern female can be nearly as tall as the gobbler but typically weighs only 8 to 12 pounds. Hens are similar in color to the males but are more brown, and the metallic iridescence is less brilliant. Breast, flank and side feathers are tipped in brown. Females lack the caruncles— fleshy protuberances of skin

About the Expert

Mary C. Kennamer, managing editor of *The Citizen News* of Edgefield, South Carolina, served as information specialist for the National Wild Turkey Federation for 17 years. She is also an avid turkey hunter, having shot both Eastern and Rio Grande subspecies.

In her work for the NWTF, Kennamer produced bulletins on the five subspecies of wild turkeys that inhabit the United States—the Eastern, Florida or Osceola, Rio Grande, Merriam's and Gould's—as well as another species of turkey, the ocellated. Much of the following profiles are adapted from those bulletins, with the permission of Kennamer and the National Wild Turkey Federation. The bulletins, in their entirety, are available from the National Wild Turkey Federation.

commonly called wattles—at the base of the neck; the tom's wattles turn bright red when he is sexually aroused.

Beards and spurs are secondary sex characteristics in males. About 10 percent of hens have beards, but these beards are usually thinner and shorter than they are on the males. Though uncommon on females, spurs are usually rounded and poorly developed when they do exist.

In the Eastern's southernmost range, its reproductive cycle begins in late February or early March. It begins in April in northern habitat. Increasing daylight triggers the mating instinct; warm temperatures can speed up and cold snaps can slow down the cycle. The hatching of poults accordingly will vary usually from south to north from June to midsummer, and hens who renest may not bring off that brood until August.

Day-old poults learn to respond to the hen's putt, or alarm call, by running to her or freezing in their tracks. By their second week, the poults are able to fly short distances. By the end of the third week, poults can roost in low trees, which helps protect them from ground predators. This also begins a phase of development in which plants become a more important food source than the insects that had been the staple of the young poults' diet. Poults that live through the first six weeks have a reasonable chance of surviving to adulthood.

By fall, the young males and females have identifiable plumage and have established a pecking order within the flock, though they're still dominated by the brood hen. At this time, males will leave the brood group to form their own social units, and both males and females are ready to enter the social organization of the surrounding population.

Mating, nesting and development are generally similar for all the subspecies.

Diet is widely varied, but one study summarizes that Eastern turkeys in the northeast eat hard mast such as acorns, beechnuts, black cherry pits and ash seeds; soft mast such as dogwood and grapes; grains such as corn and oats; and grass, sedge seeds, leaves, other green forage; and insects. A study in the Midwest comes up with fairly similar results, concluding, "Turkeys are opportunists, eating whatever acceptable items are most available at different seasons." A study in the South indicates that when grass seed and insects become less available, turkeys shift in the fall from fields and pastures to forests for mast.

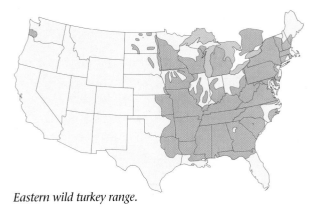

Eastern wild turkey range.

~~~ FLORIDA ~~~
(Meleagris gallopavo osceola)

The Florida wild turkey, also known as the Osceola after the Seminole Chief Osceola, is found only on the peninsula of Florida.

Though similar in appearance to the Eastern wild turkey, there are indeed differences. The Osceola is smaller and darker with less white veining in the wing quills. The white bars in its wing feathers are narrow, irregular and broken, and do not extend to the feather shaft. Black bars predominate in the feathers. Secondary wing feathers are also dark, and when the wings are folded on the back, there are no whitish triangular patches like on the Eastern.

A Florida turkey's feathers are more iridescent green and red, with less bronze, than the Eastern's feathers. The dark color of the tail coverts and the large tail feathers tipped in brown are similar to the Eastern's, unlike the lighter colors of the three western subspecies. Adult hens are similar to the males, but a female is duller and lighter-colored except for her wing feathers, which are actually darker than a tom's. The Florida's coloration is suited to the flat pine woods, oak and palmetto hummocks and swamp it inhabits.

The reproductive cycle begins only slightly sooner than that of the Eastern subspecies in Southern states; however, in southern Florida, the adult males may be gobbling in January, several weeks before mating. Egg laying takes place mainly in April, with the cycle complete and peak hatching in May.

One study of 32 birds between October and February indicated 114 different foods, but 10 foods made up more than 90 percent of that diet. In fact, pine seeds and acorns comprised almost 70 percent of the diet. Other major foods were grass seeds and leaves, cabbage palm, black gum seeds and corn.

Florida wild turkey range.

The Slams

Successfully sport–hunting a gobbler of any subspecies is an achievement of which a hunter can be proud. Some people choose to hunt turkeys beyond the borders of their home state or province. A hunter who harvests each of the main four subspecies in the United States—the Eastern, Florida, Rio Grande and Merriam's—is said to have accomplished the Grand Slam. The Grand Slam can represent a lifetime achievement, but the ultimate is getting all four subspecies in one spring.

A hunter who adds a Gould's to a Grand Slam has shot a Royal Slam. Finally, a hunter who gets all five of those subspecies and also harvests an ocellated turkey is said to have achieved the World Slam.

RIO GRANDE

(Meleagris gallopavo intermedia)

The Rio Grande wild turkey—namesake of the river on the Texas/Mexico border—is native to that region, up through central Texas and the central plains states. This is the turkey of arid and relatively open country, and its taxonomic name suggests an in-between appearance between the eastern and western subspecies.

The Rio Grande resembles other wild turkeys and is about the size of the Florida turkey, though its legs are longer. Comparatively pale and copper colored, the Rio's tail feathers and tail/rump coverts are tipped with a yellowish-buff or tan rather than the medium or dark brown of the Eastern and Florida. Feathers of the breast, sides and flanks are tipped with pale pinkish buff. Rio Grandes can grow up to four feet tall. Hens weigh from 8 to 12 pounds, toms around 20 pounds.

The Rio inhabits brushy areas near streams and rivers as well as mesquite, pine and scrub oak forests in the arid regions of the southern Great Plains, West Texas and northeastern Mexico. You can find Rio Grandes at elevations as high as 6,000 feet; they generally favor more open country than their Eastern and Florida cousins.

The Rio is nomadic, traveling several miles a day to feed, but it usually returns to its favored roosts at nightfall. When tall trees are not available, it might roost on a structure like a power line or windmill.

Rio Grande turkeys sometimes establish a separate winter range and have even been known to form flocks of several hundred birds during winter. Rio Grandes tend to choose the tallest tree near a stream or in a deep valley for a winter roost site. Gobblers, especially, choose such areas as roost sites year-round.

The Rio Grande is not adaptable to treeless prairies or vast spaces between wooded areas. For one thing, it lacks coloration for concealment and is too large to hide in grassy vegetation. Where hardwoods from stream zones have encroached onto the grassland, favorable habitat has developed, aided by the advent of livestock farming and the control of prairie burning.

Rios have been introduced into the dry summer habitats of the West's lower elevations in Nevada, Oregon, Washington, Wyoming, Utah, South Dakota and California. They have also been transplanted into greatly differing habitats, such as northern Idaho and Hawaii.

Breeding behavior begins while the birds are still in their winter flocks. Mating activities often occur in open areas such as roads, pipelines, power line rights-of-way and areas with naturally short herbaceous vegetation.

Like their cousins, Rio Grandes eat a wide variety of foods. A Rio's diet includes grass and forb leaves and seeds, insects, soft mast, hard mast, grains and prickly pear seeds.

Rio Grande wild turkey range.

—ᴟ— MERRIAM'S —ᴟ—
(Meleagris gallopavo merriami)

The Merriam's wild turkey—named for C. Hart Merriam, first chief of the U.S. Biological Survey—is primarily a denizen of the ponderosa pine regions of America's Western mountains.

Though its suspected historic range was Arizona, New Mexico and Colorado, the Merriam's has been successfully introduced to other parts of the Rockies and to Nebraska, Washington, California, Oregon and other areas. The Merriam's normal range receives annual rainfall between 15 and 23 inches, indicating the birds' preference for relatively arid habitat.

Adult males are distinguished from Eastern, Florida and Rio Grande toms by the nearly-white feathers on the lower back, as well as the white tail feather margins.

Comparable in size to the Eastern, the Merriam's appears blacker, showing blue, purple and bronze reflections. It appears to have a white rump, due to its pinkish, buff or whitish tail coverts and tips. The males exhibit black-tipped breast feathers; the females' are buff-tipped. The white areas on the hen's wings are more extensive, giving a white appearance when folded.

Some Merriam's turkeys migrate considerable distances—up to 40 miles from Rocky Mountain foothills to higher elevations—for breeding and nesting, then return to lower elevations for the winter. Snow conditions, food availability and the presence of suitable roost trees may dictate the migration.

When long periods of deep snow prevail, turkeys can be forced into riverbank habitats below the coniferous zone. There, turkeys might use cottonwoods for roosting and may become dependent upon barnyards, grainfields, silage pits and feedlots for sustenance. The movement away from wintering areas, back toward breeding and nesting grounds, usually occurs between mid-March and mid-April.

Similar to other subspecies, the Merriam's is an opportunistic feeder, eating seeds, leaves of grasses and forbs, fruits of shrubs and vines, mast of pine, oak and juniper, and animal foods including insects and snails.

Merriam's wild turkey range.

GOULD'S

(Meleagris gallopavo mexicana)

Nonhuntable populations of Gould's may be found in New Mexico and Arizona. Hunted in northern Mexico, this subspecies is named after J. Gould, who first described the bird in 1856.

Like the Merriam's, the Gould's is a bird of the mountains. The largest of the five subspecies, the Gould's resembles the Merriam's but has longer legs, larger feet and larger center tail feathers than any of the other wild turkey subspecies. Gould's turkeys have white tips on the tail feathers and tail rump coverts. Lower back and rump feathers show copper and greenish-golden reflections. Body plumage may be described as blue-green. Adult females have a less-pronounced greenish/reddish sheen, tending instead toward a purplish appearance.

The center of the Gould's range is Mexico's Sierra Madre Occidentals. Populations exist in the states of Chihuahua, Sonora, Sinaloa, Durango, Zacatecas, Nayarit, Jalisco and Coahuila. Small numbers also exist in a few mountain ranges of southwestern New Mexico and southeastern Arizona.

Gould's populate north-south running mountain ranges with elevations ranging from 4,500 to 6,500 feet in the U.S. and more than 9,800 feet in Mexico. Their territory features hot summers and mild winters, where the average annual precipitation is about 18 inches, more than half of which falls between June and September. Habitat in Mexico is similar, though it is prone to more severe winters because of the higher elevations.

Water is a key habitat component and a limiting factor in the Gould's range. The existence of livestock ponds and watering facilities is sometimes their only source of water.

The Gould's gobbling activ-

Gould's wild turkey range.

ity has been documented to begin in April or May in Mexico and from late April to June in New Mexico. The gobbling seems to coincide with plant green-up in the birds' range. The gobble itself is of a lower frequency than either of the two other western subspecies.

In its habits, the Gould's turkey is similar to the other subspecies, with a couple of exceptions. First, when hens search for a nest site, they seek a nearby water supply. Second, the alarm putt a poult hears from its mother is a much higher-pitched vocalization, which sounds more like "pitt, pitt."

Acorns, grass seeds and leaves become more important foods after the young birds' diet switches from insects. Studies also show the importance of juniper, pine, wild cherry and blackberry in the uplands and palms, palmettos, figs, other plants, insects, tender green leaves and grain in the lowlands.

The Ocellated Turkey
(Meleagris ocellata)

*M*eleagris gallopavo—the species of turkey comprised of the five subspecies of North America—is only one of two species of wild turkeys. The other species is *Meleagris ocellata*, or the ocellated turkey. Called by other names throughout Central America (*pavo, pavo ocelado* or its Mayan name, *ucutz il chican*), the ocellated turkey exists in portions of southern Mexico, northern Belize and northern Guatemala. Its range is actually a 50,000-square-mile area encompassing the Yucatán Peninsula of Mexico, northern Belize and the El Peten region of northern Guatemala.

These birds look quite different than their northern cousins. Body feathers of both sexes show a mixture of bronze and green iridescence. Females typically appear duller, showing more green than bronze. Unlike the subspecies to the north, breast feathers are the same on both sexes, and neither sex sports a beard. The tail feathers of both sexes are bluish-gray, with an eye-shaped, blue-bronze spot near the end, followed by a bright gold tip. Its fanned tail might remind a hunter more of a peacock than a wild turkey.

The ocellated's upper secondary wing bar is a rich, iridescent copper. Barring on the primary and secondary wing feathers is similar to North American turkeys but contains more white.

The head and neck of both sexes is blue, with orange to red, wart-like growths called nodules. The male's head has a fleshy blue crown behind the snood, which is adorned with yellow-orange nodules. During breeding season, the crown enlarges and the nodules become more pronounced in color. The birds also have an eye ring of bright red skin, which also becomes pronounced in the male during the mating season.

Though the ocellated turkey's legs are shorter and thinner than its northern counterparts, the males' spurs are longer and sharper, averaging more than 1$\frac{1}{2}$ inches for males older than a year. Spurs as long as 2 inches have been recorded.

In general, ocellated turkeys are smaller than any birds from

the *Meleagris gallopavo* species' five subspecies. A hen's weight peaks at about eight pounds during nesting and remains around 6 or 7 pounds during the rest of the year. The tom weighs between 11 and 12 pounds during the breeding season.

Ocellated turkeys simply sound different, as well. A series of three to seven low-frequency, hollow drumming sounds precedes a high-pitched gobble. The drumming, similar in sound to that made by ruffed grouse, seems to replace the pulmonic puff (a low-pitched "humming" or "chumping") given off by North American gobblers.

Some of the species' vocalizations are indescribable, though one of their sounds can be likened to a nasal cluck. The cluck serves both as a locating signal and an alarm call. Studies on this species are limited but suggest that, perhaps because of the many predators in Central America's tropical forests, the ocellated chooses silence over vocalization in order to survive.

The ocellated's habitat includes arid brush-lands, savannas, marshlands, second-growth forests interspersed with abandoned farmlands and old-growth mature rain forests.

Mexico does hold a nonresident spring gobbler hunting season, which usually runs from late March or early April to late April or early May, with a bag limit of one. So there is a chance for the adventuresome turkey hunter to bag an ocellated turkey.

Ocellated turkey range.

Chapter 2

DREAMING & PLANNING

irst, you must get the fever. Be warned: It's easy to catch!
Usually, exposure to a thundering gobble or the sight of
a turkey in full display—tail feathers fanned, chest puffed out
and wings flexed—is enough to infect you with the bug. Beware:
There is no known cure, and the fever never really breaks. Turkey
fever is chronic, lasting typically as long as the person who has
contracted it does. The only way to treat it is to go turkey hunting, as often as you can, in the magnificent spring woods; add
some autumn hunts, too, if you can.

Sure, there might be spells when the symptoms subside. But
when a hint of spring shows itself with a warm breeze, or your
lawn shows a richer green than winter's dormancy, things will
start to get rolling again. A television hunting episode or the
chance sighting of a roadside wild turkey on a wintry day while
you are driving to work will also heat up the fever again.

Old-timers in-the-know suffer the worst. Their past experiences—a love affair, you might say—kindle the fever's flame. At
least those veteran hunters know what they will be doing before
the season begins, and what they learn from their preseason
work will direct them to possible locations on opening day.

But new hunters, and others looking for more successful out-
comes to their days afield, can benefit greatly from those who
know the ropes. So in the pages that follow, you might first catch
the fever or, if you're already infected, you'll enjoy a relapse.
Then learn the first step in the prescription for a successful recovery from Bill Hollister, a man who has combined a career as a
wildlife biologist with a lifetime of woodsmanship and decades of
turkey hunting experience. Discover what you can do to get
started—to find land to hunt, close to home and far away; to
find where the birds should be; and to find out exactly where
they are.

These are the first steps, backed up by years of positive clinical
results, in a treatment program for wild turkey fever.

THE ALLURE OF TURKEY HUNTING

First I heard the faint sound that jerked my head erect. If my ears could move like a dog's, they would have aimed themselves toward the distant squawking. The *we-onk* had already begun to stir my soul when the aerial honking grew louder. I shielded my eyes with my cupped hand across my forehead as I scanned the cloudy skies for the source of nature's music. Once more, I

heard the squawking, this time louder, giving me a new reference point. Then I saw it—a classic V. The Canada geese were heading south.

No sound ever stirred my soul like the calling of Canada geese—until I heard my first gobble from a wild turkey tom. If you've heard it, you know that your ears are not the only part of your body affected by the thunderous outburst. The gobble vibrates through your stomach, tickling every nerve in your midsection, and then winds up in your heart, which seems to bolt toward your throat. The call of the wild tom is at the heart of turkey hunting; it is a sound and symbol of that which is wild. And it represents something that man has restored to numbers unequalled in the last century.

Those who do not hunt might presume that the kill is what makes the hunt a success. But those of us who have sought the wild turkey know the many sources of pleasure long before we pull the trigger; these pleasures are just as strong on the many occasions when we never even get off a shot.

First, there's the countryside. Everyone has his or her own favorite scenes in the outdoors. One of mine is looking over a green field surrounded by stands of thick forest. Turkey hunting brings me to the tall ridges, where high-mountain breezes swirl about as I look across a sunken valley to hillside fields and greening woods. In the autumn, those woods are ablaze with fiery red, golden, yellow and brown leaves.

Fields of prickly pear cactus in South Texas are another stroke of nature's artistry. So is a greening cornfield—flanked on all sides by mixed hard- and softwoods—in western Iowa, or an open meadow tucked into the pine and spruce elevations of South Dakota's Black Hills. These are the types of places that host you when you pursue the wild turkey.

If it weren't for turkey hunting, many sportsmen would find little motivation to walk the spring forests, though the visual rewards are unique. Spring is when spotted fawns are being dropped, birds are sitting on nests and other young are first seeing the world. Spring is when I once watched an auburn whitetail doe and a wiry

About the Author

*G*lenn Sapir is author of this book. His passion for outdoor writing is perhaps exceeded only by his love for turkey hunting. As an outdoor communicator, he has served on the editorial staffs of several outdoor magazines, including *Field & Stream, Outdoor Life, Sports Afield* and *New York Sportsman.* In addition, he contributes articles on outdoor recreation to a number of magazines, including *North American Hunter* and *North American Fisherman.* His magazine articles and photographs have received several awards.

Sapir has been hunting wild turkeys since 1980, pursuing them minutes from his home in the Hudson Valley of New York, and in several states across the country. Sapir recently accomplished the Grand Slam of turkey hunting, bagging Eastern gobblers in New York, a giant Florida in the Sunshine State, two Rio Grandes in Texas and a Merriam's in South Dakota. Having hunted with many of the experts in this book, he has witnessed their talents firsthand. He knows the others included in this volume by the tremendous reputations they have carved.

raccoon feed along a Florida slough; it is when I had the honor to see three red fox kits stare curiously outside their den at my hunting partner and me on a rocky New York hillside.

You may set out on your own, of course, but

Turkey hunting takes you into beautiful country, offering a variety of majestic big-woods and agricultural settings.

other good times together, or work or school or maybe family. Turkey hunting is always a relaxing outing with good talk. Back at camp you'll discover that the relationship has grown more special by sharing time afield.

And of course there is the gobble, that unique call of the male turkey that reverberates through the woods. It is an unforgettable entrance into the world of the wild turkey and a signal that you are within earshot of the prize you seek. The tom's tipoff, however, is only the beginning. Now you must figure out whether to get closer or stay where you are. You must decide whether to sit against the nearby large oak or move to the lip of the ledge on which you are standing and find another structure against which to prop and hide yourself.

The decisions have just begun. Shall you call or be quiet? If you call, which caller will you use? Who will call? And when the bird has been quiet for a long time and has not shown itself, should you stay or move? Many quiet toms mere yards away have been spooked by hunters who have chosen to get up and move. On the other hand, stubborn gobblers have often been outsmarted by hunters who know it's time to move, reposition themselves and attempt a different calling strategy.

For those who love a challenge, the wild turkey is *always* a worthy adversary, and anyone who thinks his strategy and skills are foolproof is only fooling himself.

But turkey hunting's strongest allure is anticipation. Whether you are a deer hunter, a bass fisherman or a turkey hunter, the greatest excitement in the sport may likely occur in the moments before you down your game or net your fish.

If you're a deer hunter, what can be more exciting than sitting in your treestand and hearing the still quiet of the woods suddenly being broken by the swishing of crinkly autumn leaves that carpet the forest floor? The noise gets louder. The hairs on the back of your neck stand up. You know a deer is near and, by the ever-louder sound of the leaves, that he's getting closer. Somehow you know it is a buck. With your heart pounding so loud you think the buck is going to hear it, you slowly raise your rifle or bow, knees shaking. And

you are just as likely to share turkey camp with others. With eyes half-closed, you fumble side by side in the predawn hours, trying to jump-start your body and prepare for the ensuing hunt. You skulk through the woods together, perhaps one a veteran turkey hunter and the other a not-so-experienced one.

Parents set out with offspring. One may do the calling, the other the shooting—or you may pool your calling talents. You'll whisper stories while you walk or while you sit and wait. These stories may be about previous hunts—like the one last spring when you missed the huge gobbler—or there he is … steadily walking your way, head down. The breeze is perfect as you concentrate on his shoulder and not that dark, thick rack.

If you're a fisherman, picture yourself driving up to a bass pond with your small boat in tow. You've never fished this little lake before, but you've heard rumors that lunker largemouths abound. You survey the pond from the shore: The close-to-shore waters are littered with blow-downs, stumps and lily pads. You rig a couple of rods, putting a favorite surface chugger on one. Then you ease your boat into the water and sneak up on the most fishy-looking spot you've ever seen.

You cast your chugging plug just beyond a large stump. It sits for a few seconds, though to you it seems like minutes. Finally, you raise your rod, gurgling the lure up to the stump. Suddenly, the water erupts, as if a stopper were just pulled beneath the lure, and the chugger vanishes as you set the hook.

In the first scenario, you have not yet released the arrow or pulled the trigger. In the second, you have not yet netted the bass. Yet the anticipation

Parent and offspring create special memories together afield.

and action leading up to those moments may be the most thrilling aspects of the experience.

So it is with turkey hunting. First comes the excitement of knowing what might follow— when you set out in the early morning darkness,

First you probably detect motion, then you focus on the tom—his tail feathers fanned, his chest puffed out and his wings flexed. This is hunting excitement at its best!

Dreaming & Planning

shivering as much from the excitement of the moment as from the predawn chill. You owl-hoot and hope to shock a tom into gobbling. He does, and you head in his direction, knowing that the bird you desire is here. You stop by a large tree—and quietly listen. This time the gobble is louder, and it has resulted from no call by you. This bird is announcing to the world that he is ready to share himself with any hens nearby.

Anxiously you set up a decoy or two, then settle down against a wide tree that will hide your outline. Light is beginning to break through the dark skies, and songbirds are welcoming the new day. You wait, then give a soft tree call. Another gobble thunders forth in response. The minutes slowly creep by, then you pull a trick out of your bag, taking off your cap and beating it repeatedly against your thigh, imitating the sound of a turkey flying down from roost. And you wait some more.

A minute later you hear a similar flapping of wings. The gobbler has landed. You make a series of soft yelps and receive an answer: a gobble that pierces your clothing and rattles your innards. Then another, even closer!

Without moving your head or any other part of your body, your eyes scan the vista before you. You wonder whether your shaking will subside when you want to steady your shotgun, which is now propped on your knee and pointing toward the sound of the last gobble.

Then you detect motion ... first the patriotic head, painted in a pattern of red, white and blue. Then you realize the gobbler has fanned his tail feathers, puffed out his chest and lowered his wings like flexed biceps—showing off for the hen that your deceptive calls and wing beats have portrayed.

Have you ever seen a bird so beautiful—or so big? The tom looks huge, even compared to the geese you have hunted. Heck, he's almost as tall as a deer's shoulder. *Why won't he come closer?* you wonder. Perhaps he wants this hen to come to him, the way nature usually portrays this mating game. So you stay quiet for several more minutes as he struts back and forth, never getting any closer. Though you hate to use your hands to call at such a close distance to the tom, you pick up your rounded slate and ever so softly emit a tantalizing purr.

The gobble is so loud it is frightening. Your call has done the trick! The big tom is coming so fast that he's almost running. He stops one more time and goes through the display ritual again, raising his neck to scan for your presence. He takes a few steps behind a tree, giving you a chance to aim your gun where he likely will be when he clears that oak.

Now it is time to release the gun's safety and pull the trigger. Inexplicably, the shivering has subsided. You have anchored your right arm on your right thigh, your left on the other leg. The bead rests where you think the bird's head will appear.

When you set out with a companion, you might discover by day's end that the relationship has grown stronger.

He steps out from behind the tree, and you gently squeeze off a shot.

The bird drops and starts flapping, so you spring from your sitting position. In a heartbeat—miraculously, your heart hasn't stopped—you are looking down on your bird as its last seconds of life leave its feathered, beautiful body. Before you is a giant turkey, one that you have called in and shot.

The congratulatory handshakes back at camp await you. The special dinner that offers a unique link to the meals of our nation's forebears will also follow.

But for now you need to fight the shakes that have returned. You take a deep breath, look around to relive exactly what just transpired, then go back to admiring this magnificent gamebird.

It's time to head back to the vehicle or to camp, so you unload your gun, tag your bird, tuck the great gobbler in your vest, walk over to your decoys and put them back in your vest as well. Then you set out, carrying a lot more weight than you did when you entered the woods—but somehow the experience has given you new strength, and the extra weight feels oh so good!

This is only a taste of turkey hunting, and the surprises and challenges you'll encounter in the woods and in yourself are unpredictable. The opportunities abound; the rewards are countless.

Dreaming & Planning

STARTING OUT

$\mathcal{E}$xperts throughout this book will help you get started. They'll help you learn to call. They'll tell you what accessories to bring on a hunt. They'll even tell you what to wear. But the best calling while you're donning the best-equipped hunting vest and wearing the most effective camouflage clothing won't do you much good if you don't know where to find the turkeys.

LOCATE A GENERAL HUNT AREA

"Contact the fish and wildlife agency in the state you want to hunt," recommends Bill Hollister. Having worked at such an agency for 33 years, this accomplished turkey hunter knows just how helpful personnel can be.

"Obtain harvest records for the various counties in the state and see if the agency representative can help you pinpoint hot spots. A lot of times, when an area continually leads a state in turkey kills, it not only means that it holds a lot of turkeys but that there may be a lot of public hunting land available and perhaps a minimal amount of 'No Hunting' postings on private property."

"Once you get some idea of where to hunt in that state, contact the agency's regional office covering that area," advises Hollister. "Talk to a biologist or a technician who is familiar with the area. Find out what public land is available for hunting. Ask for maps of public lands—state and national forests, for example, and public state-managed access areas."

This is a very important step. Why? Because while personnel at headquarters can probably give you good information on general trends, the field office personnel really get out to their region's turkey country to see what's going on.

Studies have shown that agricultural areas, mixed with timbered lands, can be ideal habitat. And dairy farms, especially in the Midwest and Northeast, are real hotbeds for turkeys, Hollister says. "Dairy farms usually grow grains for cattle feed," he explains, "and turkeys love that. When the farmers spread manure over the fields for fertilizer, the undigested food that has passed through the cattle helps sustain the turkeys all winter."

GAINING ACCESS TO PRIVATE LAND

Hollister likes to get permission to hunt on areas that are actively farmed, commenting, "I like to drive the roads in rural areas and look for land that seems to have oak ridges, especially red and white oak, interspersed perhaps with farm fields. If there are not actively farmed fields, I look for fields in second growth where soft

Take advantage of any opportunity to glean tips and advice from local folks and game department personnel.

mast—everything from winterberries to black cherries and chokecherries and gray dogwood berries to grapes—is available."

"It was once believed that you needed 5,000 acres of unbroken stands of mature hardwoods to support turkeys. Now we know that small wood-lots adjacent to farmlands and fields hold very good numbers of wild turkeys," says Hollister.

Once you've located lands that show promise, the trick is getting access. "My advice, generally, is to contact the landowner well before the season and be extremely courteous." Hollister feels strongly that the contact should be made in person.

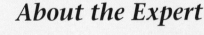

About the Expert

*B*ill Hollister has combined his hunting skills and woodsmanship with the professional knowledge gained in a long career as a biologist to become a highly successful turkey hunter. In fact, Hollister spent 33 years on the staff of New York's Division of Fish, Wildlife and Marine Resources.

He understands the turkey and communicates his knowledge well. He currently is a professional outdoor writer and photographer, and his work has appeared in a number of magazines. Hollister has conducted many seminars on hunting the wild turkey and has had a hand in television, film and radio productions in which his outdoor expertise was key. He even has judged turkey calling contests in six states, including two U.S. Open Turkey Calling Championships.

Dreaming & Planning

Once you've gained permission to hunt on private lands, you will find that courtesy and respect for the property earns great dividends in the form of helpful information.

"Present yourself in street clothing rather than camo," he proposes. In your first contact, you might not even ask permission to hunt, Hollister notes. "Talk with the landowner about his property and the wildlife on it. At times, I've first asked just for permission to photograph the wildlife. I've taken pictures of the wildlife, including turkeys, on the property, and I've blown up the photos and presented the landowner with some of them. That will lead me up to a request to hunt the property. Photography has helped me get access to some lands."

Sometimes, besides asking well ahead of the season—"January or February for the spring season and during the summer for the fall season"—offering to help in some way can be a key as well, suggests Hollister. "Perhaps you could offer to help post the land or lend a hand in some other way."

"My son Jim and I hunt a piece of property that we were given permission to hunt. We noticed that an old logging road that went into the property had several potholes. Jim and I actually went out and bought stone and spread it on the road. We improved access for both the landowner and ourselves."

"Now," Hollister adds, "we have almost exclusive use of that property." That's one of the joys of getting access to private land. You can experience virtually untapped turkey resources without competition from other hunters. And you'll probably make a new, good friend in the landowner to boot.

Once you have permission to hunt, respect the landowner and his property. Hollister, for instance, makes sure not to shoot within a proper distance of the residence. "Ask the landowner where to park your vehicle. Make sure you don't block roads and farm lanes." Let him or her know in advance when you will be hunting on the land and what kind of vehicle you will be driving, especially if it is one the landowner is not used to seeing you drive. "Those subtleties show a landowner you respect him and his property," Hollister remarks.

Of course, you aren't always going to get permission to hunt. "If you get a 'no' answer right off the bat, be polite to keep the doors open. But don't give up." In the meantime, send a note thanking the landowner for his or her time. Offer to help with haying or fencework, or do the milking a night or two to give the landowner an evening off. Then, Hollister suggests, "Ask the landowner again at a later time. He may have softened up." It truly is work to get access to good land, but the payoff is well worth the effort.

GUIDED HUNTS

If you are hunting outside your local area, someone else can help pave the way to hunting access. "Sometimes, by going through the National Wild Turkey Federation to get a local contact in the area you wish to hunt, you may get lucky and find out about private lands to which you may get access," Hollister points out.

Of course, not all hunting is a on a do-it-yourself basis. State fish and wildlife agencies can direct you to guides and commercial turkey-hunting camps or even to state guide and outfitter associations where they exist. Advertisements in hunting magazines present another way to become familiar with commercial opportunities.

"It's a more expensive option, but often the extra bucks are very well spent because you connect with somebody who has been out in the woods, has done some scouting, knows the area and has access, and can put you onto birds a lot more readily than if you were doing it on your own."

Before You Book—Ask Questions!

Whether a guided turkey hunt introduces you to some great new country or a whole new subspecies you have not yet hunted—or even helps you "learn the ropes" from a seasoned turkey fanatic if you've never hunted turkeys before—it will definitely be an adventure you'll remember for a lifetime. But adventures can be good or bad. To make sure your hunt is a positive experience, ask questions like these when you're selecting an outfitter and checking out references.

For an outfitter:

- What are the accommodations? Are they included in the price?
- Who does the cooking?
- Are we hunting private or public land? (Get an idea of hunting pressure—you want as little as possible.)
- What are the benefits/drawbacks of different hunt windows? (Decide whether you should go early, late, first-second-third season, etc.)
- Describe the hunting style. (Does it match your abilities and commitment?)
- Describe your guides and their experience.
- Are licenses awarded via draw, or are they over the counter? Who applies—you or me?
- What is your average success for: getting shots for clients; harvesting birds?
- What is and is not included in the price? (Airport pick-up and return, bird cleaning and processing, etc.)
- What would I bring? (Get a list.)
- Please provide a list of references, both successful and unsuccessful hunters.

For a reference:

- What did you think of the accommodations and food?
- What's your opinion on the quality of the land hunted? (Number of turkeys, hunting pressure, etc.)
- What time during the season was your hunt?
- Did your guide know his stuff, work hard to get you onto birds?
- Did you have chances to get birds?
- Did you get any birds?
- Would you go back there again? Why or why not?

—Tom Carpenter

Dreaming & Planning

One method of preseason scouting: Call from country roads that border potential hunting grounds and listen for responding gobblers.

When contacting a commercial guide or lodge, you need to ask some questions to determine whether it is the option you wish to choose. Hollister advises, "Ask how much land is available. Find out if there is access from the private land to public lands. Determine what sort of success rates hunters at their camp have had. Also, ask for references—a list of satisfied hunters who have hunted with them. Then call some of the people and discuss their experiences with the outfit. Obviously, the guides are probably not going to give you the names of people who were dissatisfied, but say you want to talk to hunters who did *and* didn't bag birds."

SCOUTING

If you're going on a guided hunt, much of the preliminary work will be done. Obtaining permission or finding some good public land to hunt might be the toughest part of getting started on a successful turkey hunt if you're doing it yourself. Yet permission doesn't guarantee success; nor does finding good public land. Scouting then becomes key.

Says Hollister, "During the months of March and April, before the New York season opens in May, at dawn and dusk—much more at dawn than dusk—with a box call handy, I'll drive the backroads bordering the properties I know I can get access to hunt. I'll be listening for gobblers on roost. I don't do too much calling, and when I do, it is with the box call, a gobble, or locator calls such as an owl hoot or goose call just to get the birds to respond. I just want to know they are there, not have them come to me yet."

"Of course, I will also walk the ridges, hoping to hear a gobble from a remote hollow. I'd rather hunt one of those birds, maybe by himself, that you can't hear from the road. I'll have less competition hunting him and he will not have heard many calls. The birds that I hear from the road may have sounded off for other hunters who practiced their calling on them and even called them in before the season—not a good idea."

When Hollister walks those ridges, he looks for gobblers, of course. But his eyes are wide open for much, much more than just a wild turkey. "I'll look for sign. I'll look for scratching—where leaves have been turned over and the soil raked by feeding turkeys. Most of the scratching you'll see in the spring is made by hens because the gobblers feed very little then. They have built up a fatty breast sponge, which sustains them while they devote the spring to breeding."

A turkey dusts—scratching and flapping its wings to create a lot of dust—to rid itself of pesky bird lice. Look for these dusting areas when scouting.

Distinguishing Male & Female Sign

When Bill Hollister is scouting for turkeys before the season or hunting during the season, he always seems to have at least one eye on the ground. He knows that clues to a gobbler's presence might be lying right in front of him. There are ways to distinguish a gobbler's sign from a hen's. Here are Hollister's tips:

SCRATCHING

"I've read this and proven it to myself: Gobblers scratch close to the base of trees. The scratching you see in the spring in areas away from the base of a tree could be either sex—though most likely hens, since they feed more than gobblers do during the mating season. But scratching near the base of a tree has likely been done by toms."

FEATHERS

"Dusting areas, where turkeys wallow in the dust to help rid themselves of bird lice, can reveal a variety of sign suggesting which sex has been there. Tracks, droppings and feathers are there. The body feathers of a hen have buff-colored tips; a gobbler's has shiny black tips."

DROPPINGS

"A female's droppings are kind of round. They seem to pile up and form a round blob. A male's droppings (shown) are larger—the diameter of a piece of chalk—and more 'J'-shaped."

TRACKS

"The size of tracks differs between a hen and a tom, and so does the stride between tracks. From the back of the track to the front of the center toe, a gobbler's track will measure more than $4^1/4$ inches, a hen's less than $4^1/4$ inches."

Dreaming & Planning

Hollister also looks for dusting areas—bare stretches of soft, dry earth that might resemble a buck scrape. At times, turkeys will also dust on old ant hills, he explains. "Turkeys scratch and flap their wings in the dusting spots to create a lot of dust, especially underneath their wings, where bird lice tend to be. Almost all turkeys have some lice on them, and they dust to rid themselves of the pests."

Another key sign to success is locating roosting trees. To find them, pinpoint their location by listening for gobbles at dawn and dusk: Seeing birds go to roost, actually being on or coming off roost are the best ways to identify an exact tree. You can also identify roost trees by a collection of droppings on the ground below their limbs, Hollister says.

Yes, turkeys leave clues to their whereabouts. Sometimes the hints are audible, sometimes visible. Gaining access to property they inhabit is the first challenge, then finding and putting the clues together is the next. When starting out, if you can successfully combine those two challenges, you have, indeed, become a turkey hunter.

Two keys to turkey hunting success: access to good turkey country and proper scouting. Both are hard work, but the rewards are great.

Dreaming & Planning

Chapter 3

SELECTING YOUR GEAR

*I*f there was ever a sport made for mail-order catalogs, it's turkey hunting. Aficionados drool over the featured selections, and every time a better mouse trap appears on the pages of catalogues or on display at local sporting shops, these hunters are ready to throw down their hard-earned cash.

What gear really works? What do you really need? And most importantly, how do you use the products to become a better turkey hunter?

If you are wondering about the answers to those questions, you are in luck because assembled here is the collective advice of people who know the answers. In fact, many of these experts—Mike Jordan of Winchester, Chris Kirby of Quaker Boy, Ronnie Strickland of Mossy Oak, Eddie Salter of Hunter's Specialties and Dave Berkley, founder of Feather Flex Decoys—have earned their livelihood by knowing what's best for the turkey hunter. The others, John Miller and Larry Townsend, have demonstrated their skill and knowledge on every one of their frequent hunts.

Whether shotgunning is your approach, as it is with most turkey hunters, or you choose a less typical arm to chase your gobbler— bow, muzzleloader or modern rifle—understanding what to use and how to apply it to turkey hunting is a necessity.

If the advice were as basic as which kind of shotgun or type of bow to use, this section of the book would be short and simple. But selecting an arm is only the beginning. Discerning what staples and accessories best complement them is an equally important ingredient in the mix. Yet the greatest tips that come from these experts' wisdom reveal how to assure yourself of getting the best results from the combined use of essentials and accessories.

You'll learn about clothing from head to foot, calls, decoys and turkey hunting vests and the cargo they should carry. If you could ever hunt with any of these mentors, you would appreciate the skill that backs their words. But since you won't likely be going afield with them, then at least you have their knowledge for company. It may prove to be the most valued companion you've ever hunted with.

SHOTGUNS & AMMO

"When it comes to choosing your shotgun," says Mike Jordan, "you have a wide selection. In choosing an action, for example, go with whatever you are most comfortable with."

Jordan points out considerations that go into selecting an action. "Keep in mind that if you are going to shoot the heaviest loads, use a semiautomatic because it can absorb a lot of recoil. Though you are likely going to use only one shot to kill your turkey, you are going to fire several shots in patterning your shotgun. Even a good single-shot could work, but the most popular are pumps and semiautomatics."

You can even use double-barreled side-by-sides and over-and-unders, Jordan admits, but if you plan to camouflage these more expensive types of shotgun permanently, you might decrease their value.

Jordan also believes that several different gauges are effective—from .410 up to 10 gauge, but he acknowledges that 12 gauge is by far the favorite. "The 12 gauge offers a lot of pop and is accommodated by a really wide selection of top-notch loads. Those who choose 20 gauges and .410s really lessen the distance at which they can cleanly kill a turkey. This puts a premium on hunting and calling skills to bring the bird within 20 yards."

When it comes to choke, Jordan is far less liberal in allowing choices. "Full or extra-full will keep your pattern tight. Turkey loads respond to choke very well, and with a tight choke, you can maximize the number of pellets in your target's lethal zone."

Another detail to consider in shotgun selection is barrel length. "For turkey hunting, 22 inches would be minimum and 26 inches maximum. Anything longer than 26 starts getting in the way and can make it hard to swing past limbs and brush for a shot. A 22-inch barrel creates an awfully powerful muzzle blast, so I would rate a 24- or 26-inch barrel as ideal."

About the Expert

An indispensable part of all turkey hunters' gear is their shotgun and the loads hunters choose to shoot. Mike Jordan, manager of public relations at the Winchester Division of Olin Corporation, knows that it is essential to have the right gun and loads, but he also recognizes that a lot of different models and brands could fit into that "right" category.

CAMOUFLAGING THE SHOTGUN

Action, gauge, choke and barrel length are important specifications to consider. But so is appearance. "A shotgun should be camouflaged,"

Turkey Loads: An Analysis

Gauge	Shell Length Inches	MM	Dram Eqiv.	Muzzle Velocity Feet-per-second	Shot Charge Weight Ounces	Grams	Shot Size	Pellet Count
Tungsten-Iron Turkey								
12	3	76	3 3/4	1300	1 3/8	38.98	4	192
High Energy Lead Turkey								
12	3	76	Max.	1300	1 3/4	49.61	4	236
							6	394
Magnum Lead Turkey								
10	3 1/2	89	4 1/2	1210	2 1/4	63.78	4	304
							5	382
							6	506
12	3 1/2	89	Max.	1150	2 1/4	63.78	4	304
							5	382
							6	506
12	3	76	4	1175	2	56.70	4	270
							5	340
							6	450
							7 1/2	700
12	2 3/4	70	4	1250	1 5/8	46.06	4	219
							5	276
							6	366
20	3	76	3	1185	1 1/4	35.44	4	169
							5	212
							6	281

Selecting Your Gear

Camouflage a shotgun with paint, tape or a "sock" that slips over the gun. A helpful accessory is a camouflage sling. To reduce the chance of telltale sling movement, you can unsnap the sling when setting up on a hunt.

advises Jordan. "Today, you can buy a lot of shotguns already camouflaged at the factory, but if your gun doesn't come that way, you have many options on how to do it."

"Simple, removable paint that you can pick up at an archery shop will work. Or there are several sleeves that will fit over a gun. I had a gun that wasn't available in camo, so I sent it to RealTree

A center bead is important as a sighting aid, assuring proper alignment as you aim.

and they dipped it. It came out really well."

Another method of camouflaging shotguns is with a nonadhesive camouflage-pattern tape that is secured by an adhesive such as electrical tape.

"If you don't have your gun camouflaged, then try at least to make it not shine. Many times it is that last motion, trying to move the gun into proper position, that gives you away. Talk to a gunsmith about giving your gun a matte finish."

SHOTGUN ACCESSORIES

Beyond the actual firearm itself are a number of shotgun accessories that can help make it the complete turkey gun. "I really like slings," Jordan declares. "There is often a lot of walking involved, as well as calling to try to locate birds, and you can get around quicker and easier if you are not carrying your shotgun or if you don't have to lay it down each time you want to call."

One important tip to keep in mind from Jordan: "If I'm working a turkey, I will usually unsnap the sling and just lay it across my lap so that the bird can't detect its movement as I raise my shotgun for the shot."

Slings that slip over the stock and muzzle of the gun serve the purpose, but they may block the front bead when you aim your gun, and they would have to be removed when you are setting up on a bird. "I like the slings that attach with a swivel," says Jordan. "They stay out of the way and are easily removable. Foam slings are very comfortable and quiet and seem to soak up some of the gun's weight."

Most shotguns have a bead, and for many turkey hunters, that's all the sighting help they ask from their shotgun. But Jordan thinks they should ask for more. "At the least, a gun should have a front sight and a center bead that allows you to line up your shot and make sure that you don't raise your head while you are shooting."

Jordan finds even more aid from red-dot sights and scopes. "They really make you focus on squeezing the trigger until you've fired. In turkey hunting, you don't jerk the trigger; you squeeze it like a rifle. If you keep the red dot at that crosshair on the target, that's where it is going to hit. And the scope gives you an added advantage: You can really look the bird over and see what kind of beard it has."

A low-power scope is all you need for turkey hunting, since range is relatively close. "A scope that varies from $1\frac{1}{2}$ to $4\frac{1}{2}$ power would be fine," Jordan advises. "You'd generally have it on the lower end, probably no more than 2 to $2\frac{1}{2}$ power."

SHOOTING

Unquestionably, the most important aspect of selecting a shotgun is using one that will shoot where you want it to shoot, within a reasonable

Patterning Your Shotgun

atterning a shotgun is the routine of firing a shotgun at a target to determine the performance of a certain load. What you are looking for is location and density of the shot.

"Start off with a full-size turkey head target," recommends Mike Jordan. "These targets are available at most shooting supply stores, and you can easily make copies of them for future use. I also like to mount the target on a 4-foot-square sheet of cardboard or paper so I can see the whole pattern."

"Create a situation where you can hold the gun steady so that you know performance is due to the combination of the gun and the load, not you. To start, you might even begin with a lighter load than you intend to use, just to make sure your point of impact is where you want it to be. With heavier loads, sometimes it's harder to gently and steadily squeeze the trigger because of the fear of recoil."

"Begin with several shots at 25 yards to make sure you are on target. Then switch to the load you intend to use. Statisticians say you need 25 shots for scientific conclusions, but practically speaking, once you switch to the heavy loads you intend to use, you don't want to shoot each load more than two or three times at each range. Then back up to what you think your maximum yardage for a shot will be and move in 10 steps. Take a few more shots to make sure you've got good coverage there and your point of impact is still good. You need at least four pellets in the lethal head and neck area."

"If your gun isn't shooting where you are aiming, you have two choices: You can correct it or you can allow for it."

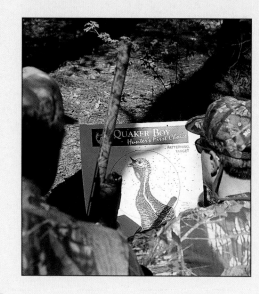

In other words, if you know that your gun is shooting one foot to the left of where you are aiming, you can aim one foot to the right of where you want your shot to hit.

"But allowing for it is always risky in the heat of battle," warns Jordan. "You may simply forget or misjudge the allowance. That is one of the advantages of the scope or red-dot sight over a simple bead. You can adjust a scope or other sight—make the shotgun shoot where that crosshair or dot is. If your gun is still off, try adjusting the choke. If that doesn't work, go to a gunsmith." You need to be on-target, and confident you can hit and cleanly kill what you are aiming at.

Leaving your hands free without putting the gun down, a sling is particularly convenient when you stop to call.

range. "I don't recommend any shot over 35 yards," Jordan maintains. "For one thing, it is hard to judge distance, and it's easy to misjudge by 10 yards, especially under low-light conditions. If your gun is patterning well, you may still get pretty good coverage up to 45 yards, but I wouldn't want to count on a shot that far."

For a shotgun to pattern well, you need a gun that shoots where you want it to shoot, and you must have ammunition that can accomplish its task. "First of all, you need a pattern of pellets dense enough to be almost 100 percent sure that you're going to hit a lethal area. So you need a small shot, but you want a shot size big enough to penetrate the bones, neck and head once it gets there."

Tests at Winchester labs produced a surprising discovery. "Size 6 shot is the favorite shot, but the testing we did showed that beyond 30 yards, you cannot rely on it for effective penetration. Knowing what we do about hunters' frequent mistakes on range estimation, I like 5s. But they have to be in a heavy-enough load to get the pattern coverage. I would want at least 1½ ounces in a buffered magnum that really patterns well."

Like shotgun actions, size of shell is left somewhat to personal preference. "Most people use 3-inch shells," Jordan says. "More and more, how-

ever, are using 3½-inchers. The one thing I would say is that if a person is going to shoot 3½-inch shells loaded with lead, he'd better be darn sure he can handle the recoil—because it is going to be considerable. If you are using a pump-action or a single-shot, go to a range and make sure you can handle that load before you go out into the field with it. You can get into some strange positions in the field, and you might dislocate a shoulder if you can't hold the gun properly." Better to find out early on if you've got too much gun to handle comfortably.

Because of the high-velocity loads available in 3- and 3½-inch sizes, Jordan considers 2¾-inch rounds a considerable disadvantage. The most important criteria in selecting a gun and load are comfort and performance.

Jordan's final advice on selecting ammunition is simple and sensible: "Pick a load that shoots well. Once you settle on a load, try different shot sizes. And use different chokes to see what suits you best at the ranges you think you'll be shooting. After that, it boils down to a personal choice."

The best advice on selecting a shotshell load: Use at least a 3-inch shell that shoots a minimum of 1½ ounces of shot. Go to a 3½" shell only if you can handle the recoil. Whatever load you choose, pattern with it and know where it hits.

Hunting With Rifles

*T*hough turkey hunting is thought of as a close-range shooting sport in which a hunter tries to call the bird within shotgun or bow range, there are many parts of the country where turkey hunting is also a rifle hunter's game.

"Riflemen are deer hunters," reports Mike Jordan. "Many of those riflemen, especially in the West, would much rather go after a turkey with a rifle than with a shotgun. It's spot-and-stalk hunting, much more like big-game hunting than traditional shotgunning. You stalk the turkey until you get into position for a good shot."

Despite the long-distance accuracy of the .22 caliber rifles that Jordan says are commonly used for turkey hunting, getting off a good shot is still not easy. "It's tough to make a lethal shot without ruining much meat. In my opinion, the ideal shot would be right where the head and body meet."

Jordan believes that a .22 centerfire bolt-action rifle proves most accurate and effective for this aspect of turkey hunting. Shots should come from 100 yards or less, he says.

Safety is a major consideration in all turkey hunting, but Jordan recognizes that rifle hunting warrants even more care. "You have to be able to identify your background," he advises. "You have to make sure you are not shooting over a hill or rise or anywhere that bullets can hit something you cannot see."

To aid in that safety goal as well as the goal of bagging a turkey cleanly, Jordan says that a scope on the rifle is essential. "The power depends on how far you're going to shoot. For close in, 4 power is fine. If you are going to shoot out 100 yards, 12 power will be great. A good varmint setup will be just fine."

The ethics of hunting turkeys with a rifle has been questioned by some. "I've heard people say that it is too easy and that it doesn't require calling," Jordan comments. "It's a different type of hunting for a different type of person, that's all. A big-game hunter in the West may get much more satisfaction making a good shot with his rifle than shooting anything with a shotgun."

According to National Wild Turkey Federation records, 8 states allow rifle hunting in spring seasons, 13 in the fall. Check regulations before planning a hunt in any state.

HUNTING TURKEYS WITH A BOW

*I*f you think bowhunting for turkeys requires some very different techniques than the approach you would take when hunting with a shotgun, you'll find one expert who disagrees. "Spring and fall hunting strategies are pretty much the same whether you are hunting with a bow or a shotgun," asserts John Miller, who has successfully hunted turkeys with both arms.

BOWHUNTING EQUIPMENT

What about equipment? How does that differ from the tackle Miller would use for deer? "If a person is an archer—I don't care if he hunts with a longbow, recurve or compound, and generally speaking, it doesn't matter which species he is pursuing—he is going to use the same equipment. The bow has to be tuned and the arrows must fit the bow. I use the same equipment whether I am going for elk, whitetails, bears or turkeys."

Though Miller believes that the same bow and arrows can work on turkeys as on deer, he does recommend a couple of modifications to your equipment when your target is a wild turkey. "I use one of two commercially–made items to help ensure my bringing home the bird. The first item is best for the novice; it's a spool of up to 2,000 yards of very strong line attached to the bow. The line is attached to the arrow. If the arrow goes completely through the turkey, which tends to happen, you are not left with just an arrow and a bird that has flown away, perhaps to die and never be found. This way you have the line to track down your bird."

Another device that Miller recommends can help prevent the arrow from hitting the bird and simply exiting. "A few different companies make a star-shaped device that slips onto the arrow behind the broadhead," he explains, "reducing penetration for a more lethal shot."

Miller does use the same bow and arrows as he does for other game, but a bowhunter after turkeys can choose to make other adjustments. One option is to use a broadhead designed for turkey hunting. It's like the standard head but features two blades that are reversed, which slows down the arrow upon impact. A second alternative that can slow the arrow is to use a bow of a lesser pull weight.

The significant difference between hunting with a gun and with a bow falls in the category of distance. "A shotgun hunter can roll the bird at 30 yards. I have to bring the bird within 15 yards when I am bowhunting."

Despite the way Miller simplifies the sport of bowhunting for turkeys, he knows that range is not the only added challenge, and he's discovered that specialized equipment and know-how can help an archer become a successful turkey hunter.

SETUP SECRETS

A bowhunter might have to remain still longer than a gun hunter while waiting for a shot, requiring him to stay put in one position for a longer time. Also, getting the shot off will create more movement than pulling a trigger, so a bowhunter has to maximize concealment and comfort.

One bit of gear that Miller deems indispensable is found more often in a ballplayer's locker than in a hunter's equipment duffle. "I always wear knee pads that are elastic around the knee," he reveals, "because most of the time when I am bowhunting, I am on my knees. When I'm standing, I'm still very comfortable. And with the knee pads I can kneel for 25 minutes without pain. Without the pads," Miller says, "every rock, twig and other object would dig into my knees, making it uncomfortable and not allowing me to kneel for very long or stay as still as I'd like to." He dyes the knee pads green for camouflage purposes and wears them over his pants.

Another bit of equipment Miller considers a necessity in helping him hold his shooting position is a belt-mounted bow holder, or bow holster. Miller describes it as a loop that goes on

---

About the Expert

John Miller is highly regarded for his hunting skills. At age 14, Miller made his first bow out of lemon wood and deer hide—a replica of those used by Native Americans along the Delaware River—and became hooked on bowhunting.

He downed his first whitetail with a bow soon after his honorable discharge from the army. When turkey hunting took hold in New York's Catskill Mountains, Miller quickly became proficient at hunting them with a shotgun, filling his spring and fall New York tags almost every year. To add more challenge to his hunting, Miller traded in his shotgun for a bow. The bow is now his arm of choice, and he has arrowed several turkeys. He hunts them in Pennsylvania, New Jersey and Montana, as well as his native New York.

A bowhunter might have to stay still longer than a gun hunter while waiting for a shot. Comfort and concealment are vital.

his belt. He rests the bottom of his bow in a little cup hanging from the loop, which takes the weight and pressure off his arm and hand. "When you wait for that bird to present the right shot, you may be holding for five minutes. There's no way you could hold your bow straight for that length of time. I keep the bow in my holder," he explains, "which is on my left side. I am a right-handed shooter, so I am going to be holding the bow in my left hand."

As mentioned before, one of turkey bowhunting's biggest challenges is getting the bow drawn without that sharp-eyed gobbler detecting the movement and spooking. Gun hunters just don't face as big an obstacle to success if their shotgun is, as it should be, pointed at where the turkey will be coming in.

The archery solutions? "I always carry small, hand-sized pruning shears," Miller describes. "That way, I can quickly cut a couple of hemlock or other branches that will hide me, stick them in front of me, and just like that I've got a blind. I also carry camo netting in case I want to use it to construct a blind. I recommend an 8-foot length of 4-foot-wide camouflage mesh.

Archery turkey hunting's biggest challenge is getting the bow drawn without the sharp-eyed gobbler detecting the movement.

Selecting Your Gear

Use pruning shears to clear shooting lanes and cut branches that you can stick in the ground for a blind.

a blind set up, the birds can't pick me out as easily when I'm shaded by a conifer's boughs as they can when I'm sitting against a wide hardwood. But any tree is better than no tree." Of course, using a tree is always good for safety too, especially if there are firearms hunters in the woods.

PRACTICE, PRACTICE, PRACTICE

Before you ever take to the woods with your bow in pursuit of a wild turkey, you owe it to yourself and your game to prepare properly. "A bowhunter must practice to gain proficiency," Miller urges. A turkey is smaller than a deer, and the kill zone is tiny when you get right down to it. Killing a turkey with an arrow is a huge challenge.

"I don't like using bird targets, but for a novice I recommend them. You have to get an idea of the anatomy of a bird so you know where to put that arrow. The chest area is where you want to put that arrow, though you may get lucky and hit him in the neck and still kill him," Miller points out. "The actual size of a turkey is about a third of what you might think it is. You are looking at all of those feathers on a bird that weighs 22 pounds and stands almost 4 feet tall and 1½ feet wide. But I estimate the true kill zone is only about 6 inches around and you've absolutely got to know where it is."

Here's how Miller translates that into specific shots at the turkey, depending on the angle. "My favorite shot is when the tom is fanned and is facing away. I aim to hit about three inches above the bull's eye—that's right, his anus. The arrow will go right through his vitals and out toward the chest."

"If I have a side view," Miller continues, "I look for the color change on his wings. I pick a particular feather and aim for that. When I am practicing, I'll put a leaf on the board and use that for my target. When I'm actually shooting at a turkey, I'll pick a spot on the side that is dead center of the bird. The tighter the focus of your concentration, the better off you are. If you shoot simply at the entire bird, you'll miss."

You can fold it into a 6-inch square, put it in your game pocket and hardly even know it's there until you need it."

Though Miller knows that you don't always have the option, when a good-sized evergreen tree is in the area in which you wish to set up, use it as your backrest. "Whether or not I have

Practice diligently with your bow, and work on picking a specific spot in which to slip your arrow.

BOWHUNTING STRATEGIES & TECHNIQUES

So you've taken up the challenge: Your bow is tuned; you're confident you can hit a turkey's small vital zone; you know where you're going to hunt. How do you go about getting a gobbler within bow range? It's not easy. Remember: In general, the bird must be even closer than he needs to be if you were carrying a shotgun.

First of all, Miller says decoys can be a big help. "The ideal situation is to roost a bird—that is, locate the spot where he has flown up in a tree to spend the night (see pages 108–109 in 'Locating Turkeys,' chapter 4)—either in the spring or the fall. If I know where a bird is roosted, I can create a blind nearby. I'll come back before first light the next morning, and from the blind I can try to call him in after fly-down and take my shot."

"I'll have a couple of decoys set up, closer in than I might with a gun. The decoys help distract the gobbler, giving him something to focus on. The decoys also might make the gobbler fan out. I like to have my decoys face me.

That way, the gobbler will probably want to face the decoy and put his back to me. Then he gives me that bull's eye I like to shoot over, presenting what I consider the most lethal shot."

A bowhunter is not going to be sitting down while all this action is taking place. "I'm either standing or kneeling. I never move if that bird's head is not looking away or covered by a fan. When the gobbler comes in with a hen or hens, I have more sets of eyes to contend with. Not until the bird or birds go behind a tree or are turned away from me will I go to full draw."

This is a critical point in your hunt. More turkeys escape bowhunters by detecting the movement of the hunter's draw than any other aspect of the hunt. Never underestimate that turkey's ability to catch you cold if his eyes are exposed in any way to your movement. Multiply the number of birds you're facing and the challenge becomes even greater.

Bowhunters after deer consider treestands almost essential, but they don't necessarily work for turkeys. "Bowhunters will be more successful if they hunt strictly from the ground," Miller advises. "Turkeys are very

A decoy can distract the gobbler and help create an ideal shot for the bowhunter.

Selecting Your Gear

Though makeshift foliage and camo netting blinds are more common, portable blinds can also be an aid. The key is giving yourself a better chance to draw your bow unobserved by sharp turkey eyes.

adept at picking out odd-shaped forms in trees. Deer have had to evolve into animals that look upward for danger. But turkeys, from the day they are born, have to fear predators from above—like hawks and owls—so they are used to looking up with suspicion."

THE LAST WORD

In addition to the combination of right archery gear, equipment to make the hunter more comfortable and better concealed, and a knowledge of the bird's habits and anatomy, Miller says the successful hunter needs one more special ingredient. "A bowhunter has to have confidence, and that comes with the best preparation a person can give himself. Attitude is everything."

Are the rewards of bowhunting worth the sacrifices of putting aside a "long-range" shotgun? "You are choosing to put limitations on yourself. If you were out there just to fill a tag, you wouldn't be bowhunting. It's not the most efficient way to harvest game; we all know that. It gives you more challenge, and successes are all the more memorable. To succeed gives you a special satisfaction. Even if you don't get a bird, you'll observe more wildlife and turkey behaviors than you ever imagined. I've had birds at 30 yards or more that I could easily have taken with a shotgun, but then I wouldn't have gotten to study them and watch the way they behave."

Arrows: Shot Placement

When you have a shotgun in hand, deciding where to aim is a done deal: You shoot at the turkey's head. The spread in your shot pattern—even with the tight choke you should be using—gives you a little margin for error and the pellets will do an effective job penetrating that unfeathered head for a good kill.

An arrow presents some interesting contrasts: Even though it's not propelled by a charge of powder, an arrow penetrates turkey feathers with ease, compared with lead shot. But that head—what a tiny target to hit with a single arrow! So, placing your archery shot requires some different thinking.

John Miller's favorite shot is when the tom is fanned and is facing away. He aims to hit about three inches above the bottom center—the bull's eye—of the fan. The arrow will hit vital organs.

When a side view presents itself, Miller looks for the color change on the wings and aims for that spot. He picks a particular feather and aims for that, because the tighter

When a turkey is facing away, aim as shown. This is an ideal shot, with the turkey's fan concealing your draw.

his focus of concentration, the more likely he is to hit the bird. "If you shoot simply at the entire bird," he says, "you'll miss."

Though not one of Miller's favorite shots, and despite the tiny kill area, some bowhunters do favor the head-neck shot, and a side view offers the best opportunity for that target.

Though Miller estimates the actual killing zone of a turkey is 6 inches around, others have narrowed that down to as little as 4 inches. In any case, it is obvious that a lot of practice and an understanding of where to aim are essential for a bowhunter after the wild turkey.

The wing shot presents the largest kill zone, but some bowhunters still prefer the head shot.

BLACKPOWDER TURKEYS

Some hunters can't wait for the next high-tech firearm, load or accessory to be invented—to make their pursuit of the wild turkey easier and more likely to end with a tagged bird. Standing proud against such a modernistic view is Larry Townsend of Vienna, West Virginia.

AN OLD-FASHIONED HUNT

"Sitting and leaning against enough trees, waiting with my modern shotgun for a wild turkey to come in, gave me plenty of time to think," Townsend recalls. "I've always had an interest in history, especially of my immediate area in West Virginia, and after missing a few turkeys and killing a few, I came to the conclusion that anybody who was halfway proficient at killing wild turkeys probably had a good shot at survival in my local wilderness during the 18th century. I wanted to see how I might have done."

So he set off for Friendship, Indiana, home of the National Muzzle Loading Rifle Association,

*L*arry Townsend was raised in Ritchie County, West Virginia, a place so rural that when a car went by, everyone would race to the window to see who it was.

Townsend grew up in the world of hunting, and his first excursion for turkeys was in the fall of 1966. That got him started, and he learned more and more—by doing, reading and watching. In the fall of 1971 he bagged his first turkey, and he's taken 51 more since then; 26 of those birds have fallen to a muzzleloader.

Townsend prizes the history of his Ohio Valley roots, and he has adopted the authentic guns and clothing of that region's 18th-century frontiersmen. His record of success speaks for the expertise he has developed as a blackpowder turkey hunter.

where most of the people in the blackpowder industry come to show off their wares. "I ended up commissioning a flintlock after talking to one fellow for a couple of hours," Townsend relates.

That began his turkey hunting with a muzzleloader. What has he found to be the attractions? "It's fun. It puts more heartbeats into the sport, and that's what it's all about. It also adds challenge—you have to take special precautions in wet weather, you are limited to shorter distances than modern 10- and 12-gauge shotgunners are, and you have a few more things to remember."

The historical attraction maintains its allure too. "I am at the point where I even carry a quill pen or an 18th-century mechanical pencil to fill out my tags," Townsend points out.

Instead of camouflage, which many modern experts deem indispensable, Townsend wears the clothing—mainly green and brown—of his designated 18th-century period. "One of the most useful garments is a waistcoat (pronounced 'whiskit'), which is nothing more than a long vest with a lot of buttons. I've already worn out one (wool lined with linen) and I have a couple more made of wool lined with wool. They are versatile and warm."

Townsend sees few disadvantages in hunting with a muzzleloader. Why? Because he views those added challenges, such as the need to shoot at a shorter range, in a positive way.

CHOOSING A MUZZLELOADER

According to Townsend, the person who chooses to hunt turkeys with a muzzleloader has three options regarding the type of firearm he might use.

"You can hunt with a flintlock, a percussion gun or a modern in-line muzzleloader," he maintains.

"On the percussion, you have an open system with a cap on the nipple. The hammer detonates the cap, sending fire through the nipple, which then ignites the main charge."

"With a flintlock, instead of a nipple, you

A muzzleloader can be an effective tool in your collection of turkey-hunting gear, adding challenge and even more satisfaction to the hunt.

have a touch hole on the side of the barrel. At the touch hole is a little pan, into which you pinch fine-grain powder. That's covered with a pan cover and frizzen. The flint strikes the frizzen, pushing it forward and uncovering the pan of powder. Sparks from the flint fall into the pan, ignite the powder and create a flash. That heat radiates through the touch hole and sets off the main charge."

"The in-line looks more like a modern gun. Basically, the improvement is that you are covering up the cap and making the gun as weatherproof as a modern shotgun."

GAUGES, CHOKES & LOADS

Once you've selected a type of muzzleloader, other options are available. "You've got different gauges—10, 12, 16, 20 and .410. I don't think you should get anything smaller than a 20. I've used a 10 gauge with a horrendous load. I've also got a 20 gauge, which takes half of that charge, and the difference in the range, in my opinion, is only about five steps."

Double guns are also available, both in flintlock and percussion, but Townsend doesn't recommend a double. "I value the lighter weight of a single barrel, and how often do you need, or even have the opportunity to use, a second shot at a turkey anyway?"

Choke is another consideration. "If you have

The blackpowder challenge embraces men and women and includes authentic muzzleloaders, replicas and modern in-line guns.

just a straight cylinder bore, like the guns of old, there is not much difference in range between a big gun and a smaller one. But that doesn't mean you can't use a choke. You can have a conventional constricted choke, or you can have screw-in chokes like in our modern guns."

"With a really tightly constricted choke, it's hard to get the proper-size wad through the choke to get it loaded. With the screw-in system, the easiest way to load the wad is to remove the choke, load it, then put the choke back in. That's time consuming and awkward, and if you want to have a gun that looks historically genuine, the screw-in chokes stick out like a sore thumb."

Townsend has discovered a way around these problems. "I like a jug choke, which is cut into the muzzle from the inside. It works well, is easy to load and doesn't show. The jug choke in my gun probably gives me 10 to 15 more steps in accuracy."

As for gauge, Townsend has taken most of his flintlock turkeys with a 12 gauge that was fashioned after an English sporting gun of about 1785. For that gun, Townsend's loads are about $1\frac{1}{2}$ ounces of number 4 shot with about 120 grains of 2F powder, the common granular choice for shotguns. "That's a fairly substantial load, but for my gun, that is safe. And I don't notice any recoil. How the gun is stocked makes a big difference in the recoil felt."

KEEPING IT DRY

Though basic turkey-hunting strategies do not differ whether using modern shotguns or muzzleloaders, differences in approach are necessary.

"For instance, you've got to keep the powder dry," asserts Townsend. "There are different ways to go about that. I use what's called a cow's knee over my flintlock. That's nothing more than a piece of shaped leather that fits

The Rendezvous

Imagine a giant 18th-century-style campout. That's the way Larry Townsend describes the modern rendezvous.

"It's kind of like a Boy Scout campout, where people camp in period-type shelters of different descriptions. Everyone cooks over open fires."

But it's more than a cookout, explains Townsend. "You visit people you haven't seen for the last year. You can compete in shoots of varying descriptions, which go on every day. There's a knife-throwing range, a tomahawk range—something is always going on."

"All the blackpowder industry vendors show up with their wares. They set up a big marquis tent for a store. It's a swap meet. Individuals like me put out a trade blanket in front of our campsites.

Anything that I have to sell or trade I just lay on the blanket. People come by, talk and see what you have."

"People dress in a historical period attire, except during the public days," Townsend added.

"There is a real big rendezvous each year—the Eastern Primitive Rendezvous—coordinated by the National Muzzle Loading Rifle Association in Friendship, Indiana. They sponsor eight regional get-togethers also."

For more information on the association and the rendezvous experience, contact the National Muzzle Loading Rifle Association, P.O. Box 67, Friendship, IN 47021, or call them at (812) 667-5131.

Selecting Your Gear

Another difference is in cleaning the firearm. "Cleaning any blackpowder gun is a little more time consuming, perhaps a bit more complicated and definitely more imperative. If you fired a blackpowder gun today and you're going to use it again tomorrow, it would behoove you to do a pretty good cleaning job because the blackpowder residue from firing it is very hygroscopic. In other words, it sucks moisture right out of the air. Clean it, make sure it is dry and don't over-oil it. On the other hand, as for getting it ready for another shot the same day it has been fired, just reload and go."

LOADING UP

Those uninitiated in the world of blackpowder shooting might wonder just how the hunt begins.

"You measure out whatever charge you are going to use and dump that down the muzzle. Then you put down one or two pieces of what's called overpowder," Townsend explains. "That's a wad of hard cardboard maybe $1/8$- to $1/4$-inch thick. Some people then use cushion wads, though I don't. Once I get the overpowder down, I just dump in the shot and then an overshot, a thin cardboard wad, to hold the shot in place."

The muzzleloader's ramrod pushes all these items into place. Townsend marks his ramrod where it clears the empty barrel so he'll always have a reference point to assure him there is no obstruction.

"The cock or hammer has three positions: fully down; at half cock, or safe; and ready to fire. Load the gun at half cock. With a flintlock, you open the frizzen, which uncovers the pan. There you put a pinch of fine-grain and 4F powder, then close the pan. Do not prime the gun until, say, you hear a turkey. Only then do you want to prime it. Note that I never prime a gun until it is light enough to see. If it's a flint gun, that pinch of powder is what I need to ignite my main charge. If it's a percussion cap gun, I don't put the cap on until it's light enough to see."

Most muzzleloading hunters aren't looking for special seasons or other favors; they simply seek greater challenges and even more satisfying rewards.

over the frizzen and covers the whole lock area. I can be in a pretty good drizzle and not have to worry about water accumulating in the flash pan."

"If the weather is really inclement, I'll slip the whole gun into a light canvas case that I carry when shooting a turkey is not imminent. When things progress, I'll take the gun out and slip the cow's knee over the frizzen and lock. At the last moment, I'll uncover it."

Misfires & Slow Fires

Unfortunately, there's no guarantee that every time you call on your muzzle-loader to do business with a turkey, things are going to unfold smoothly.

"There are misfires and slow fires," explains Larry Townsend. "Misfires can be caused by a damp or wet priming or main charge. Or you might have a dull, broken or even missing flint. In a percussion cap gun, you may have a loose or missing cap. Too much oil used in cleaning could contaminate the powder. You've got to get that oil out and be sure the barrel is dry when you are finishing the cleaning process."

"Something as seemingly insignificant as a piece of lint from a cleaning pad can obstruct the touch hole or nipple, and in a flint, you might have a wet or dirty frizzen that might not allow it to spark."

Slow fires have their causes too. "Dampness in the prime or main charge can be the problem, as can oil," Townsend continues. "Sometimes people put too much priming powder in the pan of a flint gun, or else they allow the right amount of powder, but it covers the touch hole. That will cause the gun to go off slower."

Avoiding these pitfalls is essential. In addition, muzzleloading turkey hunters can develop some habits that will help minimize the problems, suggests Townsend.

"If the touch hole is covered with powder, it creates a fuse that slows down the ignition of the main charge. So every time I sit down, I flip the gun up and away from me. That causes the powder in the pan to go to the extreme outside portion of the pan, away from the touch hole. Contrary to what some people might think, that actually allows the gun to go off quicker."

Townsend offers more advice. "One thing to remember, especially with a flintlock gun, is to keep the gun pointed at the target until the smoke clears away. Then, if you have a slow fire, you'll still be on your target until the gun goes off."

Townsend learned this lesson the hard way. "I watched one turkey for about 45 minutes," he recalls. "Actually, there were two gobblers, and the one I was watching walked up and stopped at 17 steps. It doesn't get any better than that, so I squeezed off, and the

thing went *pllltttt* and didn't go off."

"I dropped the muzzle and raised my head, which caused the turkey to fly away. Then the gun went *cabang* right in the grass in front of me. If I had continued to hold on that bird, the way I should have, I would have killed it."

MUZZLELOADING ACCESSORIES

Turkey hunters carry lots of accessories, and muzzleloading hunters add a few more that are unique to their facet of the sport.

Says Townsend, "I carry a shooting bag. You can carry anything you want in there, but you certainly need your tools. These tools include a shot pouch to carry your shot, wads, over-powder and overshot. You need extra flints if you are using a flint gun, or caps if you are using a percussion gun. And if you are using a percussion gun, you must have a capper—it simplifies putting the cap down, because when it is cold and you are a bit nervous, you'll drop more caps doing it by hand than you'll get in the gun."

"If you have a flintlock or percussion gun, carry a pick and a brush to make sure your touch hole or nipple is clear. You need a measure for measuring your powder and charges. A speedloader could be handy. You may think of speedloaders as modern devices, but there actually were speedloaders in the late 18th century."

A horn is the traditional powder carrier.

A modern in-line muzzleloader is an effective turkey hunting tool, as these results attest.

A couple of other tools to carry bear strange names. "You also need a ball puller and a worm. The ball puller is a little screw that fits into the tip of the ramrod, and the end has a wood-screw thread. With this device, you can pull balls and wads out of the barrel. It screws right into the lead ball or paper wads. You can unload the gun that way."

"The worm is a spiral-shaped wire. It originally was used for cleaning the gun. You'd wrap tow, a coarse material that is a byproduct of spinning linen thread, around the worm and actually clean the barrel with it. Even if you don't use tow to clean your gun but instead use patches, a patch may slip off the jag and lie in the barrel. A worm can retrieve it."

"Of course, you need a jag to hold the patches, and that must match your gun's gauge. You also need a cleaning brush sized to fit whatever bore your gun is."

The list of other accessories includes a screwdriver for changing flint and a nipple wrench for your cap gun. From there it is up to your imagination and your desire for pioneer authenticity. "I think it is fascinating to see what crafts people get into, including the guns and the equipment. All of it can be handmade. I make wingbone turkey calls," says Townsend. (See next page.)

"I don't know of any special turkey hunting seasons for muzzleloaders like there are for deer and elk, but muzzleloading hunters aren't looking for favors. No," Townsend concludes, "we're looking for an added challenge."

How to Make a Wingbone Call

*H*ere are instructions from expert turkey caller Bill Hollister on how to make a call from the wing bones of a turkey. This call is operated similar to most suction calls by pursing your lips and sucking inward to produce the clucks and yelps of the hen turkey. You can make this call from the wing bones of any turkey, but Hollister believes the best calls are made from the wing bones of adult hens and young-of-the-year birds taken in the fall. What a great way to use your most recent bird to help you bag your next gobbler!

① Remove the three bones in the wing of your wild turkey. Trim away the skin, feathers and flesh with a sharp knife. This exposes three bones: the humerus, the largest of the bones, which connects with the upper breast; the radius, the fatter of the two parallel bones; and the ulna, the thin bone, which will form the mouthpiece of your call.

② With a fine-toothed hacksaw, cut the bones crosswise at the locations shown.  Push out the marrow from all three bones with a stiff wire or thin coat hanger. Scrape inside of the humerus, the largest bone, with a narrow knife blade.

③ Fit each piece inside the next larger bone. Some sanding or filing may be required to obtain a good fit. An overlap of at least ¼ inch is desirable to maximize the call's strength and durability.

④ Separate the three bones and immerse them in boiling water in a small saucepan. Scrape them clean so that no flesh remains on the bones. When you have cleaned the bones well, empty the water from the saucepan, then add clean water and approximately ½ cup hydrogen peroxide. Bring the mixture to a boil and allow the bones to bleach for three or four minutes. Place the bones on a paper towel and allow them to dry thoroughly. Placing them in direct sunlight will expedite drying and enhance bleaching.

⑤ Assemble the wing bones, spreading epoxy glue on the outside of each bone that fits the  next larger bone, being careful not to get glue in the hollow portion of each bone. The mouthpiece portion of the ulna, the smallest bone, should be the narrow, somewhat flattened end.

⑥ Allow the epoxy to dry thoroughly, keeping the center bone supported. For a finished look, add white caulk to the joints and allow it to dry.

⑦ Artwork with scrimshaw or India ink adds character and beauty to the finished call.

THE COMPLETE TURKEY VEST

*T*urkey hunters carry a lot of gear. Knowing what to take and (once you've packed it) where each item is stowed takes planning and organization. Chris Kirby, renowned turkey hunter and guide, knows that his turkey vest is his portable filing cabinet: It stores his gear and offers easy access. Before he even decides what to bring along, he gives careful consideration to the vest he wears.

THE VEST

"I actually have two vests," Kirby explains. "When I'm hunting in the South or in other areas where the temperature gets really high, I usually use a vest that just has straps over the shoulders and two big cargo pockets on the sides and a game pouch in the back."

In cooler climates, Kirby's vest is more substantial, offering more pockets, compartments and warmth. "There are a lot of turkey vests out there that offer a specific box-call pouch and pouches for other calls. There's even a turkey hunter's 'belt' that offers fold-out pouches. Choosing a vest with various features is a personal choice. Most importantly, the vest has to be comfortable."

To Kirby, a vest is an organizing tool. When he is guiding another hunter, he wears a vest that can pack a lot of calls and other gear in an orderly fashion. On the other hand, if he is by himself and hunting the mountains of Pennsylvania, for instance, he thinks twice about how much gear he plans to carry. "Then I use my turkey vest as a central location for all my equipment. If the hunt dictates that I'm going to walk a lot, chances are I'll leave the vest behind and take only what I need."

Kirby acknowledges three features of a vest worth considering. "First of all, I like pockets with zippers rather than buttons or snaps. I can zip them shut and know nothing is going to slide out. Also, on all my vests, I have hunter-orange straps that can be exposed in both the front and the back. Some kind of orange device, whether it buttons on or flips out, can be a tremendous safety asset to a turkey hunter." If he's harvested a turkey and is walking out of the woods with it, or if he feels more comfortable walking around the woods with a little bit of orange, he has that added security. "It really is easy to pull those straps off when it is time to set up on a gobbler. I also usually have a hunter-orange hat in the back of my vest."

Another feature worth considering is a seat cushion that attaches to the vest. "I like a thick foam pad that snaps down. It's quick and convenient, and it's not really any extra weight."

Aside from some essential features, vest choice is a personal preference. Turkey hunters need gear, and a good vest is essential to carrying it all comfortably and efficiently.

About the Expert

Chris Kirby started his outdoor experiences at the age of five by walking the trails with his father, Dick, the founder of Quaker Boy Game Calls. Though he is the son of a renowned hunter and caller, Chris Kirby has carved his own niche in the turkey-hunting world, harvesting turkeys in 17 states. When he is not hunting for himself during the turkey season in his homestate of New York, he is likely guiding others.

Kirby's accomplishments in the field and in calling contests are a great reflection on both his upbringing and the company he helps run. Competitive calling honors include the 1995 World Championship, four U.S. Open Championships, two Masters Invitational Championships and many others. Kirby garnered an elusive title in 1998 when he won the Wild Turkey Bourbon Grand National.

You'll work your way down to what's absolutely essential in your turkey vest. Along with a compass, carrying a variety of calls is a "given."

THE CONTENTS

A turkey hunter has to decide what vest to wear, of course, but also what to put in it. "There are so many things you can throw into a vest, I sometimes think turkey hunters get carried away," Kirby remarks. He says that when he is guiding a hunter he carries a lot more calls and accessories than when he is hunting by himself. "What goes into a turkey vest is what the hunter feels comfortable using. If the vest has a spot for two box calls, does the hunter have to carry two box calls? Of course not. I tell people to go with what works best for them."

What works best for Kirby? First he notes, "I always have a compass pinned to my vest. I also always carry a small first-aid kit that includes gauze, bandages, ointments and stuff like that."

It is important to carry items for navigation and first aid and even some for survival. Kirby recognizes the worth of drinks, energy snacks, waterproof matches, space blankets that fold up to a few inches square, toilet tissue and other survival aids, but he also takes into account where he is hunting and how long he'll be hunting. "Unless I am in an area where I know I will be hunting from dawn to dusk a distance from camp or my vehicle, I travel light. On most of my turkey hunts, I'm in the woods for only a couple of hours, then I work my way back to the truck."

"Most turkey hunters go turkey hunting for three or four hours, and they don't go far from civilization. But that certainly doesn't mean that they shouldn't prepare for emergency survival situations. I do carry more in my truck than in my actual vest."

"For instance, I find an atlas and gazetteer (published by DeLorme Mapping Company) extremely helpful, especially in locating roads. A quick look at these maps will let me know how deep the woods are and whether there are any fields hidden from roadside cover, plus any other bits of important information on the area."

Kirby does carry a small flashlight, and unless the temperatures promise to be cool enough to discourage insects, he also totes some repellant. Lastly, Kirby carries a cigarette lighter. "I can always start a fire if I have a lighter with me."

Our Turkey Vest Checklist (opposite) will help you make sure your own vest is completely stocked and that you have everything you need on your next hunt.

THE CALLS

To Kirby, a champion turkey caller, calls are essential cargo for the turkey hunter, though they don't all necessarily have to be packed in the vest.

"A couple of companies manufacture diaphragm call carrying cases that you can wear around your neck. I carry mine in one of them."

A Turkey Vest Checklist

- ❏ Small flashlight
- ❏ Folding saw or pruning shears
- ❏ Knife
- ❏ Leatherman-type tool
- ❏ Compass
- ❏ Cough drops
- ❏ Insect repellant
- ❏ Compact binoculars
- ❏ Decoy(s) and stakes
- ❏ Mouth diaphragm calls
- ❏ Box call
- ❏ One-handed box call

- ❏ Slate, aluminum or glass call
- ❏ Striker(s) for the above-listed calls
- ❏ Call maintenance kit (sandpaper, chalk, small plastic bag)
- ❏ Locator calls
- ❏ Soft-pouched drinks
- ❏ Energy bars
- ❏ Toilet paper in a resealable plastic bag
- ❏ Raingear
- ❏ Shotgun shells

- ❏ Pen
- ❏ String or wire ties
- ❏ Surveyor tape to mark locations
- ❏ Pocket-size camera
- ❏ First aid kit
- ❏ Face mask
- ❏ Gloves
- ❏ Seat cushion
- ❏ Waterproof matches and/or cigarette lighter
- ❏ Space blanket
- ❏ GPS

Selecting Your Gear

No matter where he is hunting, Kirby always carries a handful of mouth calls, including some raspy ones. "Everybody has a favorite. My recommendation is to bring only the mouth calls that you are most comfortable using."

Another call Kirby always carries with him might surprise you. "I always carry a pushpin-style, one-handed box call. They are easy to use whether you've been turkey hunting your whole life or just started yesterday. It's very easy to get your clucks and purrs and hen yelps out of one of them—these are the sounds you need to bring turkeys in."

When carrying a one-handed box call, Kirby makes sure that it won't sound off in his vest while he is walking. "I flip up a sounding board and put a piece of sandpaper as a barrier between the two sounding boards. You can do the same thing with a box call. Put a piece of sandpaper or

soft cloth between the box and the striker."

Kirby also usually carries an aluminum or slate call with two or three different strikers to give him versatility. He also always carries some locator calls. "I carry a gobbler shaker, a crow call and an owl call—calls that will give me the potential to get a shock gobble."

Most turkey hunters carry a knife in their pants pocket or vest pocket or on their belt. Kirby likes an alternative. "I always have a Leatherman-type tool, which offers many more uses."

Another accessory you'll find in Kirby's vest is a container of items you might refer to as call maintenance aids. "I carry two sandpapers, chalk and a little plastic bag big enough to put my box call in if it starts raining. Of course, if there is any threat of rain, I carry rain gear."

If it is legal to use in the particular state he is hunting, Kirby also carries a decoy and decoy stakes in his vest.

Other essentials he stows in his vest are a few extra shells and a pen and string. The latter two items are for filling out and tying on a tag in states where that system exists. "A lot of states have a tag on which you cut out the date with

If you're a bit uncertain about your calling skills, rely on a pushpin-style box call. It's your best bet for producing the variety of calls you need and for making them sound good.

a knife and affix it to the turkey with the adhesive on the tag. I thoroughly appreciate those," Kirby comments.

An item that Kirby has not yet found a place for in his vest is a handheld GPS, or global positioning system; however, one may find its way into his vest soon. "When I go into an area, I may have only three or four days to hunt it. I have a tendency to stay with the easy-access places because I don't want to go way off somewhere and get lost. I think the GPS unit would give me a safety net, marking where I started and getting me back to that point."

A hunter also might think about carrying a good pair of binoculars in his or her vest, as well as a camera with which to capture a picture of the trophy in the field.

On a final note, Kirby says that he is always trying to reduce the number of accessories he carries. "When I am guiding, I bring everything I can to help my hunter get his bird," he affirms. "However, if I am going up and down mountains and back into the woods to hunt strictly for Chris Kirby, I might just bring a gun, some shells and a handful of mouth calls." When it comes down to it, hunters have to take the amount of gear they are comfortable with.

Reserve a Spot for a GPS Unit

More and more turkey vests are heading into the woods with a GPS unit somewhere in a pocket. And those vest-wearers put the units there with good reason.

First of all, a GPS unit can help you be a better hunter. One direct benefit of a GPS: In the predawn darkness it can help you find, if you're hunting big country you're not intimately familiar with, exactly where you put a turkey to bed the evening before. (See "Rise & Shine with Your GPS," page 108.)

Secondly, a GPS can help you be a more relaxed hunter, focusing on turkey hunting instead of keeping track of your whereabouts. This is an indirect benefit of having a GPS: It will give you the extra confidence you need to go the extra mile, search that far hollow, follow that roadless ridgeline, trek into that swamp, start hiking into those ponderosa foothills. You'll just find more turkeys and hunt better when you're not worrying about finding your way back to your vehicle or camp. Just create a waypoint for those key locations before you venture out.

An item that is crawling into more and more turkey hunting vests is a handheld GPS—a potential time- and lifesaver.

Finally, you can use your GPS as a scouting tool. Say you find a draw filled with oak trees on a spring hunt. Simply enter a waypoint and come the fall hunting season, you'll be able to get right back to that same spot to find turkeys feeding on the acorns that drop there. If it turns out to be a bad acorn year, keep the waypoint and visit the spot again the following autumn. Likewise, during the fall hunt or on a scouting trip, you can log in likely spots to make sure you visit them in the spring season. One of the keys to using your GPS effectively is to keep a logbook in which you record waypoints for future reference.

A lot of gear goes into a turkey vest. A handheld GPS unit might just be one of your best equipment investments.

—Tom Carpenter

Selecting Your Gear

The Well-Dressed Turkey Hunter

ry this. Ask a man in charge of public relations for a company that develops and manufactures camouflage-patterned hunting clothing what the importance of camouflage in turkey hunting is. You probably won't be surprised by the answer. But if you ask

Ronnie Strickland of Haas Outdoors (which manufactures Mossy Oak camouflage) you might be impressed by his thoughtful explanation.

"Camouflage is probably more important in turkey hunting than it is in any other sport," he begins. "Turkeys are not as smart as people

Wild turkeys are prey from the day they are born and are, therefore, extremely cautious. When you are set up for action, you are at a turkey's eye level, which makes wearing camouflage to conceal you and break your outline even more important.

give them credit for; they're just more scared. They are scared to death from the moment they are hatched because they can be attacked by a lot of predators in the air and on the ground. Owls, hawks, bobcats—all kinds of predators—are going after turkeys, so they become extremely cautious. As they move around in their daily routine, they seem to know where every twig and bush is. A deer sees a hunter and thinks it's a stump," Strickland explains, "but a turkey sees a stump and thinks it's a hunter."

"I don't know how their rods and cones are, but I'm convinced they see colors well. So camouflage can be accomplished in a couple of ways. First, you can try to blend into your surroundings, like a hen quail or pheasant does when nestled in brush. Or you can break your outline, the way a tiger with big,

About the Expert

Ronnie Strickland spends 60 days each spring in the turkey woods. Yet he hasn't shot a turkey since 1987. It's not that he's an inept hunter; rather, he is a skilled videographer, and that's what he has been specializing in ever since he helped pioneer turkey-hunting videos. Before his obsession with videotaping turkeys and turkey hunting, Strickland spent many days afield with shotgun in hand. He has accomplished the Grand Slam, and he's shot the fifth subspecies, the Gould's, with his camera.

Strickland grew up in Mississippi and hunted turkeys there when Easterns in most other parts of their historic range were few or nonexistent. Strickland's video work is only part of his responsibilities as senior vice president of Haas Outdoors, which manufactures clothing and products bearing the Mossy Oak camouflage patterns.

Selecting Your Gear

bold stripes does. Either way works, and both are necessities."

"When you are set up in the woods, sitting against a tree with your knees up, you are at eye level with the turkey—it's not like you are in a treestand—so besides wearing the right clothes, you can do a couple of things to help camouflage yourself. One is to try to set up in the shade. Even if the sun is not up yet, try to figure out where it will be shady when it does rise. The second way to camouflage yourself is to keep as low a profile as you can."

After taking those precautions, properly out-

If you are hunting areas in which the foliage will be green, make green a key component of your camouflage outfit. If green-up hasn't yet occurred, wear brown.

fitted hunters must depend on clothing from head to foot, not only to carry their gear but also to help keep them warm, dry, comfortable, quiet and camouflaged.

How Is a Camouflage Pattern Created?

Before selecting your clothing, you will probably consider the pattern of the camouflage. As you explore the variety of choices, you may

wonder about the science of creating the patterns. "When Toxy Haas [of Haas Outdoors] prepared his first pattern," Strickland describes, "he had an artist render what he wanted the pattern to be, using vertical and elliptical shapes to create an illusion and blend in. Then, after experimenting on paper with colors and variations to the pattern, he took it to the person who put the pattern on fabric and experimented with dyes and colors until he got it just the way he wanted it."

"But that was in the old days. When we began developing our most popular series, we did it by computer. We supplied a computer expert from Mississippi State University with probably a thousand slides of pictures taken in the woods and in turkey habitat from all over the country. He scanned those slides into his computer, and we selected the elements that we thought looked natural and were found just about everywhere. We ended up building our latest patterns on the computer screen, printing them out and taking them to the fabric makers."

"Interestingly, the only common element showing up in these pictures, slide after slide, was the color black—mostly shadows being cast from one thing or another."

Selecting Camouflage Colors

"Selecting the color of your camo clothing depends on where you are hunting," Strickland explains. "If you're in the South, where it greens up really early, green camouflage is really important. But I've hunted in New York's Catskill Mountains, and I know that especially in a late-arriving spring the vegetation can be mainly brown during at least the beginning of turkey season."

Though you can usually camouflage yourself in the same color and pattern from head to toe, that is not necessarily the best way to dress. "We've always preached the mix-and-match concept because it further breaks your outline. Many hunters, wisely so, wear a pattern with brown in it on their pants and use a green pattern from the waist up." These choices replicate the brown of a forest floor and the greening of the budding shrubs and emerging grass around you.

FROM HEAD TO TOE

"When selecting headwear, it again depends on what part of the country you'll be hunting. But even in the coldest areas, it will likely get pretty hot by the late season. For hot-weather hunting, I'd recommend a baseball cap that has mesh on the top and back and is camoed in front. The mesh needs to be dark- or camo-colored. For cooler climates, I'd recommend a fully camouflaged baseball cap."

Strickland says covering your face is a must for every turkey hunt. "Some caps have a netting that folds down to cover the face," he describes. "The most popular face mask is a half mask—a small piece of mesh with elastic ends. You can actually wear it around your neck while you're walking, then, when you sit down, you just pull it over the bridge of your nose."

"I prefer the head net with wire that goes around your eyes and covers your ears. You can bend the wire around the eye openings until you've shaped them for optimum comfort, camouflage and vision. There still may be a bit of your face exposed to the sun, so Toxy Haas likes to use camo paint around the bottom of his eyes and the bridge of his nose. If you have a big opening in your mask around your eyes and nose, it is a good idea for you to do the same; the exposed skin actually could shine quite a bit." If you don't like face masks, paint your face green, brown and black with a good bowhunter's face paint.

When you think about it, camouflaging your face makes ultimate sense. Why invest in camouflaging every inch of your body and then leave your face totally exposed?

Considering your clothing from head to toe also means thinking about your bottom layer of clothing. "If you think it is going to be cold in the morning, you'll want long underwear," Strickland advises. "Modern synthetics—such as polypropelene—are much more effective than old-fashioned cotton. The synthetics wick away the moisture from your body." Instead of getting the traditional white, Strickland recommends green, brown or camo longjohns. "If your pants pull up when you sit down and prop up your knees," Strickland explains, "or if your shirt sleeves ride up when you extend your arms, it could reveal your long underwear, and you don't want its color to alarm the turkeys."

SHIRTS & JACKETS

When long underwear isn't called for, Strickland recommends a long- or short-sleeved camouflage T-shirt. He also likes the idea of a properly colored turtleneck to keep you warm, if necessary, and to absorb perspiration and camouflage your neck since most shirts or jackets are open near the throat.

As for outer shirts, anything camo will work. Brushed chamois shirts are popular in cool climates, lighter cotton in warmer environs. "The regular button-up, collared cotton shirts are

A well-camouflaged hunter wears a cap, face mask, gloves, extra-long-sleeved shirts and more. Use face paint to reduce glare on any exposed skin. If you don't like wearing a mask, paint your entire face.

Breaking up your outline—here, sitting against a tree—is as important as wearing the right camouflage.

quiet. In fact, that's why cotton is still so popular. Besides the fact that it breathes, it is quiet. Bomber-style jackets seem to be the most widespread. Jackets too should have extra-long sleeves, for the same reason as the shirts. Zippers are most common; just be sure zippers aren't shiny."

THE ALL-IMPORTANT VEST

Many hunters consider their turkey-hunting vest their most important article of clothing. It is their suitcase and filing cabinet. "There are two schools of thought concerning vests," Strickland comments. "Some favor the multi-pocketed kind. We make a vest that has 22 pockets, and I'll promise you that 99 percent of the people who buy this fill every pocket. You'll find pockets specially fitted for box calls, slate calls, compasses, shotgun shells, decoys and more."

"But when you load a vest with 22 pockets, two things can happen. First of all, it can get very heavy. Secondly, you can get extremely hot because it will put more pressure on your shoulders, which will trap more heat and make you work harder to get from here to there."

Another problem with filling those many pockets is that you can forget in which pocket you put certain items. Strickland can't do much to help people's memories, but he does note that manufacturers have tried to make these multipocketed vests more comfortable by making them mesh halfway down the back for more breathability.

"The other school of thought concerning vests is to keep it simple. These hunters use a vest that is more like a game bag, with maybe 10 pockets in it. Also available is an accessory called a turkey belt, which has a wide waist strap like a fanny pack but six pockets that you can unfold when you sit down. Suddenly, you have before you your box call, slate call and stuff like that. It's lightweight and cool because you are not wearing anything like a vest above the waist."

"If you are looking for a turkey vest,"

most popular. The important thing to remember when selecting a shirt is to make sure that your sleeves are longer than normal, perhaps two inches longer." The extra length will cover your wrists, the exposed skin on your arms and any wristwatch that might be unveiled when you raise your gun to shoot.

"Over your shirt and under your vest you may need a jacket, at least in the morning when it is cool. It's important to have room in your turkey vest to roll up your jacket and/or shirt and pack them in when it gets too warm," Strickland advises. Temperature swings are often broad during turkey season; you'll want the ability to add or remove layers.

"Again, brushed chamois is very popular. The brushed chamois muffles sounds. It is very

Waterproof, camouflaged cushions may be attached to a vest or separately to a belt loop. The comfort they offer can be key.

Strickland recommends, "consider one that has a cushioned seat attached. And when you do, make sure of three things. First, assure yourself that the bottom part of the cushion, that is, the part that goes against the ground, is waterproof. Second, make sure it is camouflaged, so that when you're walking around it is not showing some bright color. Last, you also want to make sure that it can easily and quietly be put in place to sit on; snaps and zippers are more quiet than Velcro."

We could add one more feature to this vest discussion: silence. Try out the seat before you buy—really sit on it and squirm around—to make sure it won't crackle and creak loudly as you shift your weight around as you call or get ready to shoot.

If you have or buy a vest without a cushion, you can find cushions sold separately that attach to your belt. When selecting a belt to wear, camouflage may be best, but brown, dark green and other woods colors are fine. Strickland notes, "One thing many people overlook is making sure that all the hardware has a dulled finish, either dark brown or black. It's not a problem for people with a belly," Strickland jokes, "because their buckles get covered up by their shirts, but the flat-bellied types really have to be careful."

PANTS & FOOTWEAR

When it comes to pants, Strickland feels the same way that he does about shirts. Go light if temperatures allow it. He likes brushed cotton for the same reason as he does in jackets and shirts: It's quiet. And he emphasizes wearing extra-long pants, which is no surprise. "That's strictly so pants won't ride up too high when you sit down to get into shooting position."

Though hunters put most of their gear in their vests, Strickland finds multipocket pants to be very useful. "Six-pocket pants are popular with turkey hunters. Make sure pockets are flapped, snapped, buttoned or in some other way constructed to make sure you don't spill anything out of those pockets. Big buttons are good because they keep the pockets sealed and are quiet to open."

Of course, footwear is another important consideration. "If you are wearing the camouflaged turkey boots that come to midcalf, then your choice of

Multipocketed pants offer additional gear storage options.

Selecting Your Gear

High-cut boots keep you dry and offer some snake protection.

might wear for hunting that have yellow, tan, even white soles. They could prove deadly when you set up and expose the bottom of your boots to those sharp turkey eyes."

Strickland favors relatively high-cut boots—midcalf- and calf-high—made especially for turkey hunters. They are camouflaged and breathable, and if waterproof, they will allow you to wade through sloughs and cross shallow swamps in dry comfort.

Turkey-hunting boots offer several added advantages. "One benefit is that you can tuck the bottom of your pants into the boots, lace them up, spray on some insect repellant and take away the worry of insects getting into your pants," Strickland points out. "With Lyme Disease being such a problem, doing whatever you can to keep ticks from reaching your skin is important."

"These high boots can also be a savior in snake country. Most boots can't legally be called snakeproof, but these are snake resistant, and they can still be a lifesaver."

Dark-soled boots are a must for camouflage and safety.

socks is simply one of comfort because you don't have to worry about them being seen," Strickland remarks. "But if you are wearing lower-cut boots, like hiking boots, you have to wear a dark sock, preferably green or brown. The dangerous colors to wear while turkey hunting are red, white, black and blue, because those are the colors people—other hunters—associate with turkeys. Do not wear socks of these colors if your pants ride up or if your boots are low-cut."

"Because of the way socks are knit, it has proven very difficult to come up with a camouflage sock," he says. If a hunter is wearing boots that are less than midcalf in height, he should make sure that his socks are very high, so that skin or light-colored longjohns will not be exposed. "Whether the hunter is wearing low boots or high boots, camouflaged or dark brown, he needs to make sure that the boot has a dark sole. There are work boots that someone

HANDS—CAMOUFLAGE & WARMTH

Gloves can serve one or two functions, depending on the weather in which you are hunting. No matter where you hunt, gloves

Wear thin cotton gloves inside a hand muff. Your hands will be warm, and camouflaged when you pull them out.

help serve as camouflage, covering your hands. This is important because hands are the part of your body that moves the most when you are calling in a turkey. If it is cold, gloves can serve to keep your hands warm as well.

Though hunters who have suffered through the cold, early mornings of a northern turkey hunt may argue, Strickland stands firm on his beliefs regarding gloves. "You want gloves to be extremely thin, preferably cotton," he says, "so that you can run your calls, release your safety and pull the trigger. The glove should extend well over your wrist for the same reason a shirt sleeve should be long—that is, to make sure bare skin or a shiny wristwatch isn't revealed. In fact, I favor gloves with an extended wristband six inches above the wrist."

As for keeping your hands warm in cold weather, Strickland offers an alternative to heavy gloves. "Wear an insulated, camouflage muff around your waist," he offers. "You can keep your hands, in their thin cotton gloves, in there to warm. The disposable handwarmers available can also go a long way toward keeping your fingers operable. Keep a couple in your pocket or the muff."

ADAPTING TO THE CONDITIONS

Hunters know that there will be other weather conditions for which they'll have to take special precautions. "I carry with me extremely lightweight, totally camouflage raingear. It's made out of nylon and will fit in a turkey vest pocket."

"If it's extremely cold, you need an outer gar-

ment that is warm and quiet. My favorite thing is fleece. Saddle cloth," Strickland describes, "is newer than fleece and is one of the most silent fabrics for outer garments."

"An option for hot, buggy situations is a mesh jacket that is lightweight. Although it's mesh, it hides undergarments, even a white T-shirt. Some even have built-in head nets to repel insects."

Another threat besides weather is snakes. Some hunters choose chaps—available in camouflage—which slip over your belt and boots, zipping up to the top of your thighs. "But chaps are a little hot and a little noisy," Strickland cautions. "I'd rather have a high boot."

Because your hands are the body parts that move the most when you're calling in a bird, camouflage gloves are very important.

Selecting Your Gear

Washing Camo Clothing

When you buy camouflage clothing, says Ronnie Strickland, you want something that won't fade. "Look on the label to see how the dye process is done," he advises. "A vat-dying process can help prevent fading. Sure, it will eventually fade after many washings if you use hot water and bleaching detergent. The more it fades, the more ultraviolet rays it emits. If you believe, like many people do, that animals can see UV rays better than humans, you want to retard fading."

"My advice to keep your camo clothes from fading is first, don't wash them until you have to. When you do wash them, turn them inside out, zip or button them up, even shirts. Then wash them in cold water, using as little detergent as you can get away with."

ADDING IT ALL UP

From head to toe, from heat to snow, Ronnie Strickland knows about turkey clothes. He represents a company that makes them. And he's out in the woods, all across the country, for 60 straight days every year, in all kinds of conditions, wearing apparel for turkey hunting. When it comes to his suggestions, if the shoe fits, wear it.

All this seems very detail-oriented, and it is—for a purpose. When it comes to hunting and killing a turkey, success lies with the details. Attention to detail in camouflaging yourself and keeping yourself comfortable are two of the best ways to improve your chances for success.

CALLS—WHAT, WHEN & HOW

The way to a wild turkey is through its ears, and Eddie Salter knows just what to say. He's been studying turkey vocalizations since he was a kid, making his own calls, which led to a successful call-manufacturing company, competitive calling titles and trophy gobblers across the continent.

SOUNDS TURKEYS MAKE

Salter knows what turkeys have to say and how they say it. "In the spring, turkeys will make several different calls," he says. "Hens will do a cutting call, which is a real excited call telling the gobbler that they're available. That

Selecting Your Gear

About the Expert

Eddie Salter began turkey hunting at the age of eight near his home in Evergreen, Alabama.

Salter began making his own turkey calls after a few years, and that hobby eventually led to the founding of Eddie Salter Calls, Inc., in 1985. There he produced a line of turkey and deer calls, as well as scents and videos. He sold the company in 1994 and joined the Hunter's Specialties Pro Staff, and he now travels the country sharing his experience with other hunters and promoting H. S. Strut products.

Salter has proven his calling skills both in competition and in the turkey woods. He owns two world calling championship titles, and he has accomplished the Royal Slam—taking an Eastern, Florida, Rio Grande, Merriam's and Gould's turkey (in Mexico) all in the same year.

call has the most excitement of any a hunter will ever use. But what you'll hear more than any other call in the spring are simple hen yelps. You may hear from one to maybe eight calls in a row, and they may vary from fast to slow."

Another important call is the cluck. "What the cluck is doing is making a statement: 'Here I am, right over here, if you're looking for me.' That's a call the birds make 12 months of the year to communicate their location. A hunter can be successful by just learning to cluck," Salter affirms.

Even so, Salter often puts a finishing touch on a cluck with a soft purr. "On occasions when birds hang up out of range, I just give a cluck, then a little purr to give that gobbler a little bit of encouragement."

There's another call hunters might hear. "You'll also hear turkeys do kee-kees. That's the sound of a young turkey that really hasn't developed the ability to project a hen yelp. It starts off with a real high kind of whistle and then breaks into a yelp."

Salter says turkeys make other sounds—such as tree calls (which are soft yelps) and fly-down and fly-up cackles.

Salter estimates that 80 percent of the calls

you hear in the spring turkey woods are made by hens. But the call that all hunters most want to hear is the gobble from an adult tom. An adult male might gobble on his own to alert hens of his presence or to respond to a hen's call—or he might sound off almost like a reflex.

"The gobbler is all fired up in the spring," Salter describes. "Almost anything that makes a loud noise in the woods—a train whistle, a hawk, an owl, a crow—can trigger what we call a shock gobble. I think he's showing off for the hen, telling her, 'Hey, here I am!'"

Nearly 80 percent of vocalizations in the spring are hen calls.

CALLS: MATCHING THE SOUNDS

The challenge to hunters is to understand what a turkey's calls might mean, to learn to imitate and trigger these calls and to know when to use them. "The best advice I could give a hunter is to get a videotape, or even an audiotape, on turkey calling. You can learn so much by just sitting down and really paying attention."

"Then purchase the calls," Salter says. "At my seminars, I tell hunters that the first thing they need to become accomplished hunters is locator calls. The two calls I recommend are crow and owl calls. They are easy to use, especially if a person buys a can-type owl call."

Salter knows firsthand that there are many other calls that can help locate gobblers. He's heard toms gobble to wood ducks, coyotes and even blue herons, but he believes the crow and owl calls are the two with which to start.

Then Salter suggests obtaining three types of turkey calls, two of which are friction. "First, get a box call. Next, get a slate, glass or aluminum type of call. And you need to really practice with both to gain confidence in your ability. You'll discover that there are times when you use your box call and don't get any response, so you switch to the slate-type call—and connect. In general, the aluminum calls give a higher-pitched call, which could be an advantage over slate and glass on a windy day. Otherwise, it's just a matter of personal preference."

"The third call is a mouth or (diaphragm) call. Go with a light reed call with a single or double layer of latex. The back of the box that it comes in should say 'light' or 'thin' latex."

"Then go back to watching the videotape, and practice with the calls. I understand that the diaphragm call may be the hardest to learn to use, but there will be times when you have a bird out there 60 steps and you can't risk the motion of a slate or box call, but all you need is a little cluck to bring him in. That's when you must be able to use a diaphragm call."

Calls featured above include: (A) shaker call; (B) aluminum call; (C) double slate call; (D) box call; (E) gun-mount box call; (F) tube call; (G) crow call; (H) box call; (I) double-sided slate call; (J) double-sided gobbler and hen box call; (K) single-sided gobbler and hen box call.

USING A DIAPHRAGM CALL

Using a mouth, or diaphragm, call is as easy as blowing bubbles with bubble gum, according to Salter. "Put the call against the roof of your mouth, with the open part of the horseshoe toward the front of your mouth. Stick your tongue against the latex real easy, just like you were going to try to blow a bubble. The first note comes out when you start blowing against the latex. If you don't get a sound out of it, you're blowing too hard. Back up with that pressure and start blowing the reed real lightly. When it seals off the roof of your mouth, you want your tongue to go against the latex and the air to be forced out between the tongue and latex."

"Some people trim off a little bit of the tape to improve the seal. That's fine, but be careful not to cut off too much tape," Salter warns.

Salter believes that many callers, even experienced turkey hunters, keep the call too far back in their mouth. "When you do create that seal in your mouth, bring the call forward and slide it against your teeth as far forward as you can."

Salter, with his country humor, notes that there are two hazards to calling with diaphragm mouth calls. "First of all, if you keep it too far back in your mouth, you tend to gag. Second, once you start practicing and getting good, you'd better get out of the house or you are going to ruin your hopes of a happy marriage."

In a more serious vein, Salter encourages practice whenever possible. "Any time you are traveling back and forth from work, for instance, carry a call, throw one in your mouth. Chew 'em, get used to 'em. It will really help when it comes to calling for real."

Two hunters calling can get a gobbler really excited.

You should also practice under conditions that are similar to where you might hunt, Salter suggests. "If you are practicing with a friction call—a box or slate-type call—do it with your gloves on, because you are going to be wearing gloves when you are hunting. Also, get out of your house, into a wooded area if possible, and listen to your calling. The tone and pitch will be different than in the house."

USING OTHER CALLS

Although Salter knows it is a lot easier to teach someone to call in person or through a tape, there are some tips that he can pass on to help you improve your techniques with friction calls.

"Since you are most likely going to start off with a box call, you are better off if you don't pick up the lid each time you want to strike the box," he advises. "Just apply a little pressure back and forth. Don't worry about making some kind of bad call when you bring it back. You won't make any noise at all. It's when you pick up the lid for each call that you make mistakes," he comments.

Salter also has a tip for using slate-type calls.

"V" double reed.

Double reed.

Triple reed.

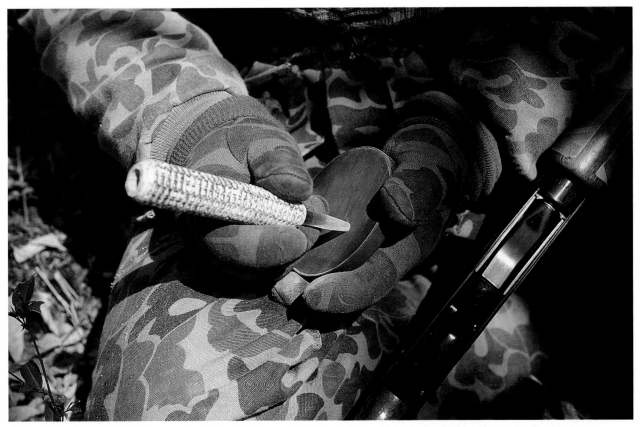

To use a slate call: Leave the peg on the slate at all times. Hold the peg at a 45-degree angle away from you, then draw egg-shaped circles in a counter-clockwise direction.

"Just like I said not to pick up the lid on the box call, don't pick up the peg from the slate call. Start your peg at the one o'clock position on the surface of the slate call, holding it at a 45-degree angle away from you. Now draw egg-shaped circles in a counter-clockwise direction. That'll get you started."

While you work on developing skills to create hen calls, don't forget those calls that mimic the gobbler. "It doesn't hurt to have some form of gobbler shaker. That is the vocalization of a tom, and you can use the call for a locator call sometimes and sometimes to work a bird."

A gobbler shaker, manufactured by several game call companies, is a tube you can hold in one hand and shake to emit a loud and authentic gobble. Similarly, you can shake a box call to create a gobble too. But using a call that projects a sound similar to that given off by the bird people are hunting can be dangerous. "But it does have its place," asserts Salter.

CALLING STRATEGIES

Though Salter acknowledges that many experienced turkey hunters carry gobbler-imitating calls, it is not what he would list as a critical call. What, then, would be the critical calls?

"The hunter would need some kind of call to do tree calling with. That's the soft, muffled series of soft yelps that would tell the old gobbler who is still on his tree roost, 'Hey, here I am, right over here in this tree.'"

"Too many hunters, especially beginners, call too much and too aggressively when the bird's on the roost. When the bird is on the roost, all I like to do is let him know where I am. If he's got hens with him on roost, I'll get a little more vocal."

"If he answers with a gobble, just answer him. Sometimes you might want to hold back and let him gobble on his own. Then come back and answer him. You be the aggressor. You can really get him fired up. I like to give him a

Selecting Your Gear

bit of cutting—a quick succession of yelps cutting into one another to let him know I am fired up and I want to see him here real bad!"

"I'll cut a few notes, then do a fly-down cackle. Sometimes I'll even take my hat off and slap it repeatedly against my chest or thigh to imitate wings flapping."

When you have a bird fired up, Salter believes, sometimes that's all you have to do to get him to come to you. A lot of hunters, even talented callers, make a serious mistake right there.

"When a turkey commits and you know he's coming in, why do you still want to call? This is where so many hunters mess up. I mess up because I love to call, I like to make him gobble, I like to hear him gobble. But if you just sit back when that bird seems committed ... nine times out of ten, he'll come in."

Sometimes it takes a gobbler shaker to get a tom riled enough to start gobbling back and coming in.

"Instead, if you go back to cackling and cutting when he is standing 75 yards away, he'll hang up and gobble. When he sticks his wings out, he's wiping the sweat off his head," Salter jokes, "because you are making him gobble too much, and he's going to wait for the hen to come to him. He won't come in any further. If you had just shut up, he would have come right in."

But Salter concedes that if you know the tom has hens with him, you do have to be more aggressive. "Then you're looking at a different ball game. Remember, I started with tree calls, then cutting and went to a flat-out cackle. When he hits the ground, if he shows any hesitation, I will aggressively hen yelp. I'll start off maybe real low and throw a few cuts into the mix. Then I'll put some real feeling into it. I start off with low cutting, then step it up. Cutting is my bread-and-butter call. It really brings him in."

Yet the gobbler may still hesitate to come into shotgun range. "If he needs a little encouragement, I might do a little cluck and purr. Sometimes I'll simply cluck to give the bird confidence. I might even scratch the leaves with my hand to make some natural sounds, or go with another call, maybe a weak purr. If he still won't come in, maybe then I'll use my gobbler shaker to let the tom know he's got competition."

But even an expert hunter knows when he's fighting a losing battle. "Don't sit there all day. If the bird has hung up for an hour, it's time to make a move. There may be a stream, ditch or other physical reason the gobbler won't come in. It may be that this is a satellite gobbler who was chased off by the boss the last time he came into a hen in that area, and he's leery."

"Move about 150 to 200 yards, then go back to a crow call. I don't feel safe using turkey calls while I'm moving. But if he gobbles to the crow call, you know where he is. Try to get all the way around the bird, pretty much in the direction he came from." Salter believes that a bird feels confident returning on a path he has just traveled.

CARING FOR YOUR CALLS

Though calls aren't expensive, you may become attached to some in particular. It behooves you, then, to give the calls the maintenance they require.

"Have some kind of carrying case for each call. That can be a pouch for slate-type calls, a holster or pocket for box calls and a little case or necklace pouch for diaphragm mouth calls. You can even use a plastic container for the slate, glass and aluminum calls. Otherwise, if you put them in your vest, they'll rub and get too slick to use."

Each kind of call warrants its own kind of maintenance. "Box calls must be chalked. Some people put on too much, and some people use the wrong kind," Salter notes. "Besides the chalks made by call companies, you can use school chalk and carpenter's chalk, which may come in the half-moon shape; they don't have any sugar in them. Some chalks, however, have a lot of sugar or oil in them, which can actually do damage to the calls."

Salter recommends a carrying case for box calls. Carry a plastic bag to put the case in, Salter says, in case of rain. That's one call that won't work when it is wet. "You can keep the box call in the plastic bag, and you can even get enough sound out of it, if the bird is fairly close, without taking it out of the bag."

Sandpaper has a place in call maintenance, but not with box calls, according to Salter. "Box calls have a beveled edge, and sandpaper might remove that bevel."

Mouth calls, too, require maintenance. "After a day or two of use, I will take a toothbrush with toothpaste and clean up my calls. I'll dry them with a towel and store them in the refrigerator, in their case, right in the egg compartment. My wife's not crazy about that idea," Salter admits, "but after 25 years she's learned to accept it." He believes it is best not to expose the calls to temperature extremes because the latex will expand and contract with the temperature changes, losing pliability and essentially self-destructing.

When a tom is close, but perhaps still out of range, don't call unless you think you have to, and then use only a diaphragm call to avoid hand motion.

The sandpaper comes into play when you are maintaining your slate, aluminum and glass calls. These calls emit their sounds when a peg or striker is scratched against their surface. When the surface gets too smooth, the striker slides against it, preventing you from creating realistic calls. "The sandpaper helps rough up the surface just enough to get the sounds you want," Salter explains.

You might read about tube calls, wingbone calls, snuff-can calls and others. They all work, and they all work toward the same results. If, however, you can understand what turkeys are "saying" and what you need to "say" to them, you can apply Salter's advice to any call—and very possibly, as Eddie Salter is fond of saying, take a tom home with you in the truck.

HUNTING WITH DECOYS

ave Berkley is an engineer, and perhaps that is why he is so logical and structured in his thinking. When he discusses decoys, for instance, he starts with the basics: what they are and what they do.

"A decoy is any object that focuses the attention of a critter," he explains. "It is designed to draw a response. The kind of a response that it elicits depends, usually, on the decoy you use,

how you use it, the situation the animal is in at the time and the animal itself. Animals are like people in that every one of them has a distinct and individual personality."

A SHORT HISTORY

When it comes to turkey hunting, decoys have found a place, and with the proper knowl-

edge, hunters will discover that different birds in different situations will require different decoying strategies. Though turkey hunting dates back to before the arrival of European settlers to North America, Berkley, who is a student of turkey decoys as well as a teacher on the subject, says there is no evidence that American Indians used decoys.

"The first turkey decoys that I've learned about were homemade models used in the 1930s and '40s. Several people from the Carolinas, in particular, described their use to me. I believe the first commercially made decoys came out of Pennsylvania. They were made by Frank Piper, though he says a larger company copied his idea the next year and started making plastic ones."

Those early decoys were full-sized turkey hens that were portable, though bulky. Today, according to Berkley, decoys can be grouped into a few categories.

"You have soft and collapsible foam, hard plastic, silhouette and a variety of movable-type decoys which can be controlled with jerk strings or electronic motors. The electronic models are illegal in some states. Actually, one state—Alabama—still bans the use of any decoys in turkey hunting. Until a few years ago, three northeastern states also disallowed decoys. I have hunted places where decoys were illegal, and I have been known to take a dried cow patty and a pine limb with a pine cone on it, which is similar to the shape of a turkey head, and stick it in the ground next to the patty. And I've had birds come to it!"

USING TURKEY DECOYS

The bans may attest to the effectiveness of turkey hunting with decoys, but a decoy is far from a guarantee of success. Using them requires an understanding of the bird you are hunting and a strategy to exploit that knowledge.

"In the spring, which decoy to use and when to use it depends entirely on the stage of the breeding cycle," Berkley explains. "I believe that a flock of turkeys goes into the

About the Expert

Dave Berkley has been hunting since childhood, though he admits there weren't any turkeys around when he was growing up in Louisiana. So he took up turkey hunting as an adult and has gained expertise to the point where he prefers to bring turkeys in close enough for him to use a .410 shotgun or a bow.

His professional background has provided an additional perspective to his turkey hunting. As an engineer who had dealt with manufacturing, Berkley's business and design talents led him into the turkey-hunting industry. In 1988, he founded Feather Flex Decoys, where he helped develop a variety of flexible, portable decoys that a hunter could easily carry by simply folding them and stowing them in his vest.

breeding cycle based on the alpha or lead hen. This timing will vary from one flock to another, sometimes by as much as three or four weeks only 100 miles apart."

"Initially, the males will be sparring, trying to achieve a hierarchy identifying which ones are going to be breeding. The competition gets more and more active and intense as spring progresses, until the ranking is firmly established and it is known which birds will be doing the majority of the breeding. So you get dominant birds, subdominant birds and birds in between. I've seen situations where, when you call to a dominant bird, he'll come in and still have two other toms with him. Those two toms will not breed; they'll stand around and watch the dominant bird breed with hens. The subdominant birds may fight each other, or if there's another male around, fight him, but they won't breed."

Selecting Your Gear

Decoys—A Basic Setup

Expected gobbler routes.

Hen decoys face away from hunter.

Jake decoy faces hunter

Sit at base of wide tree

Use decoys only where they're legal. Make sure to position them within shooting range of your location. Place the hens facing away since gobblers want to approach hens from behind. Because gobblers will approach jakes from the front to fight, place the jake (if you use one) facing you. To help conceal your position, try to keep foliage between you and where you expect the gobbler to come from. Sit with your back to the base of a wide tree for safety.

USING A JAKE DECOY

Now Berkley adds the use of a decoy to the picture. "If I am hunting a dominant bird relatively early in the season, while the pecking order for breeding is still being contested, until the hen has 10 or more eggs on the nest, I will almost invariably hunt with a jake decoy."

While at Feather Flex, Berkley developed three jake decoys—a little jake, one in half strut and one in full strut. "I believe I made the very first jake decoy. I know I was the first person to market one," he points out.

"The jake decoy elicits the response of territory. This is exactly what it was designed to do—because early in the season, territorial dominance is more important to a bird than the physical act of breeding. The dominant gobbler will go after that jake decoy to drive it off, and believe it or not, he will do it before he will ever approach a hen." In other words, the dominant bird is coming over to kick the behind of the upstart who was foolish enough to invade established turf.

Berkley recommends the jake be used with one or more hen decoys, but he is adamant that you use only one jake decoy. "The jake is the focus decoy. The tom or toms will go to the jake decoy first, and that is your aiming point. I always set up my one jake decoy in the most shootable spot for me; then I get ready, focused on that spot." You have to be comfortable: able to sit still for a long time and able to move fluidly and quietly if you need to shift positions for the shot.

"I shoot left-handed, so I want my decoy to my right at a 45-degree angle from my body, squared off to my front."

Decoys and accessories pictured above include: (A) folding hen; (B) folding jake; (C) another version of a folding hen; (D) mounting stakes for folding decoys; (E) folding iridescent hen; (F) folding iridescent jake; (G) folding jake;(H) attentive hen (doesn't fold).

Decoys — Setting up Between Gobbler and Decoy

Jake and hen decoys face hunter in this case

Hunter sets up between gobbler and jake decoy

When hunting with decoys, the standard plan is often to set up behind the fakes, in hopes of luring the gobbler right in. An alternative is to position yourself between the decoys (here, a couple of hens and a jake) and the gobbler. The idea is to get the gobbler in at point-blank range, on his way to the decoys. That's where his attention will be focused, and he might blunder right into you on his way to chase away that pesky jake. Or he could offer a shot if he hangs up, as is often a gobbler's wont.

"I want it at a range not to exceed 20 yards—because when I use a .410 I need my bird in close."

"I am a strong proponent of comfort. I find it very difficult to sit still if I am not comfortable, so I generally set myself up where I am comfortable and position my decoys to suit that setup. Most people try to set their decoys between the gobbler and themselves. An approaching gobbler's focus will be on the decoy, so I would rather be between the turkey and the decoy. In that way, I have had birds walk to within inches of me without paying any attention to me. Their focus was on the decoy."

"Believe it or not, I may place my hen decoys 50 or 60 yards away, my idea being to achieve visibility for as far as I can. But the jake decoy is always close to me. He's the point that gobbler will be focusing on and strutting to."

Using a Hen Decoy

If you are hunting the giant, old-timer gobbler of the area, Berkley believes that might be the situation to leave the jake decoy in your vest. "Everybody says the old birds are difficult because they're so smart. I have a different take on this: It's not that the birds are so smart; it's that they don't want to get their butt kicked. They might even roost a distance away from the hens and jakes. They want to avoid confrontation, and if they hang around with other gobblers, there's going to be confrontation."

"When the older birds see another gobbler, they usually go in the other direction. So, if you are hunting an old bird, never use a jake. The old bird will probably avoid it. The single hen decoy, on the other hand, can invite and hold his attention." The single hen provides an exciting enticement—one available for breeding but not associated with a bunch of other male birds to fight.

Decoys in Autumn

Testimonials from hunters around the coun-

For safety's sake, sit with your back against a tree that is wider than you are. To be perfectly safe, you would then set up the decoy in front of another tree. Most hunters, however, place their decoys in the open to make it easier for a tom coming in to your calls to notice the dekes.

try confirm the effectiveness of decoys when hunting in the spring, but what about their value in the fall? "You can use decoys literally on any and every occasion in which you are fall hunting, says Berkley. "In the spring, you may find birds that ignore decoys or are even scared by them. But in the fall, the decoys become a rallying point for every bird—gobblers and hens, jakes and poults. The reason that they are so effective then is real simple: The birds are congregated in large groups, and

Bowhunting With Decoys

Hen decoys
face turkey

Gobbler's Path

10 yards

Jake decoy
faces hunter

A ground blind (approximately 3 feet tall) allows a bowhunter to shift ever-so-slightly into position to shoot an approaching gobbler. Any leaves you rustle with your boots will sound like your decoys are feeding. You can even move your toes to sound like a turkey scratching to feed.

The decoys will help draw the gobbler's attention from you. A good time to draw is when a gobbler turns and conceals his head behind his fanned tail. You will kneel and shoot over the top edge of the blind. (It's almost impossible to shoot a bow while sitting on the ground.) And practice, practice, practice before you hunt!

"When I'm hunting with a bow," relates Dave Berkley, "I may be using two hens and a jake decoy. I'll place the jake—and I use only the little jake, that is, not one in half or full strut—10 yards away. I make sure the decoy is facing me, to the extent that I put sticks on each side of the decoy to keep it in place. This way, when the gobbler confronts the decoy, he'll likely do it face-to-face and, thus, face away from me. When he is looking at the decoy and away from me, I can go to full draw without being detected."

Berkley has some more advice for bowhunters. "Never set the decoy down-hill from yourself in that turkey-decoy confrontational situation. It should always be uphill or level, never downhill. In the downhill position, the turkey can see over his tail, and he could see you draw. On level ground, he won't see a thing. Go to a full draw; then you can take a heart shot, which is a fine shot, but my personal favorite is a head shot. I will alarm–putt, then take the shot."

"Turkeys seem to be left-handed, that is, the initial move of every bird I've tried this alarm-putting strategy on has

been to the left. The bird moves 90 degrees and stretches its head upright, seemingly frozen. My aiming point is just behind the eye."

they're looking for others of their kind. You probably first connect with the birds with some calling. Then they see the decoy, and that becomes their focus, and they will move toward that decoy. The kind of decoy you use probably is not terribly important. If you can get a little movement out of the decoy, however, it makes it much more effective."

BE SMART, BE SAFE

The most important concern in any turkey hunt is safety, and using a decoy does present a new set of safety considerations. "That's one big reason I like collapsible decoys. They are easy to conceal while you are transporting them," Berkley advises. "If you have a decoy that is an identifiable hen, or has the full body shape of a turkey, use a bag or some kind of covering over the decoy while you are carrying it."

Where you place your decoy can be another safety consideration. "The simple fact of safety is a physics lesson: Shot flies in a straight line," Berkley declares. "That means that you never want to be on the same line as somebody shooting at a decoy. Always sit with your back against a tree that is wider than you are. To be perfectly safe, you would then set the decoy in front of another tree."

Most hunters, however, position their decoys in the open, away from trees, to maximize the visibility of their decoys. Feather Flex Decoys has experimented with decoys that bear hunter orange to increase the safety factor. While the orange distinguishes them as a phony to the human eye, many birds seem to ignore the color and still get fooled by the decoy.

That's the idea of decoys—to fool the turkeys—and according to Dave Berkley, you don't need a decoy to shoot a turkey, but it sure can help, especially if you know how to get the most out of it.

Chapter 4

HUNTING STRATEGIES, TECHNIQUES & TACTICS

*T*he *successful* turkey hunting experience requires planning. That planning may begin at a kitchen table covered with maps and notes, long before you step into the cover you expect to hunt. It may end at that same table, with a collection of empty but used plates that a short time before were piled high with wild turkey meat and the proper accoutrements.

How you approach that first step and how it leads to the last requires several steps in between. Careful preparation in selecting places to hunt, locating birds, setting up on the birds and moving to better position yourself all are aspects of the complete plan.

If getting a Grand Slam is an indication of an accomplished turkey hunter, then how about some advice on selecting your destination from a blue-collar hunter who waited until mid-hunting-career to shoot his first turkey and subsequently has accomplished many Grand Slams, including a couple years of double Grand Slams? Another expert, Dick Kirby, has more than 20 Grand Slams to his credit and has accomplished this with bow, muzzleloader and pistol, as well as shotgun. Do you think he might be able to offer valuable advice on locating birds? Harold Knight, half of the famed Knight and Hale twosome, has 44 years of turkey hunting experience from which you can glean tips on setting up for your approaching turkey.

The level of expertise here continues when Ray Eye tells you how to deal with the wide variety of weather conditions you might encounter, or when Bill Hollister lays out a successful approach to hunting turkeys in the fall—a whole, new ball game from the one the spring turkey hunter is used to playing. And Steve Barras shares an unusual tactic he has developed on many of the successful turkey hunts he's made in 30 different states.

The tags these folks have filled attest to the productivity of their strategies. Here's how you can adapt their tips to your hunting strategy.

LOCATING TURKEYS

Dick Kirby is constantly afield during the turkey hunting seasons. In fact, he has hunted in 36 states, so if there is anyone who can outline successful strategies, tactics and techniques for how to locate turkeys, it is Kirby. So what advice can he give when asked how to go about locating turkeys?

"Don't make generalizations for the whole continent. It's different in every section of the country," he advises. "Where you locate the birds is different, where they roost is different and what makes them sound off could be different too."

LOCATING FEEDING & ROOSTING AREAS

The first thing you want to do is find roosting and nearby feeding areas, Kirby recommends. It's your best ticket to finding a turkey because the one thing the birds must do every day is feed and drink.

Locating turkeys yourself is one method. Getting help from others can often be easier. "UPS, other couriers and rural mail deliverers driving the roads can tip you off; so can people who

work on roads for the county, trash collectors, milk truck drivers, snowplowers and school bus drivers. Farmers, ranchers and other landowners can also be a great help." In short, anybody who travels backroads in turkey country is a candidate for helping you locate turkeys. Don't be shy. Ask!

"In the West, turkeys often roost near the ranch houses, because that is where the highest cottonwoods are growing." You'll also want to look in the riverbottoms ... places less arid than the rest of the countryside and usually treed as well. "During the day, the turkeys might gather where the cattle are fed, looking for overflow feed. In states like Nebraska, South Dakota and Wyoming, you may see flocks of 300 turkeys feeding in such areas. Under the trees where they roost you might find droppings piled 4 inches high!"

"They'll feed on seed from cow plop and in the open pastures on grasshoppers. Since tall trees may be limited in some parts of the West, you may even find birds roosting on high-wire stanchions. One fellow would watch television in late afternoon to early evening. When his reception became poor around dusk, he knew a resident gobbler had flown onto his antenna for the night. So in the pretty much wide-open West, where you find tall trees you'll find turkeys."

Things change a bit when you begin to hunt the hills. "Normally, those turkeys are going to roost in the ponderosa pines and feed along the canyons' ridgetops."

In the arid Southwest, water and food make up the key combination you are seeking. "Water is critically important. I guarantee that a water trough during the dry season will attract turkeys. Now I don't support hunting over such a spot, but you might want to get within 200 yards or so and call them."

The South has its own unique roosting areas.

Turkeys need watering spots, especially in the arid west.

Locate roosted birds using two senses: Look for sign and for the actual birds, and listen for calls and wing beats.

"In the Deep South the turkeys often are going to roost around clearcuts or over water, like swamps. If it's a dry year, they'll roost around the ponds

A locator call, often a predator sound, might draw a gobble.

that have dried up. You'll find the same favored areas in the pine woods."

"I've found the same thing to be true in northern California. That is, that the turkeys want to roost up high. It's only in the Northeast that it isn't necessarily the case. Though they often do go up high, it seems that the main thing for turkeys in that region is to stay out of the wind."

One generalization that Kirby makes about finding roosting birds is that even if you take a gobbler out of a particular area, you'll likely find more there the next year. "I think it is much like buck scrapes. You can shoot a buck over a scrape, come back the next year and find a fresh scrape in the same place. Turkeys will often roost in the exact same areas in which their predecessors roosted." The principle is the same whether it's a buck deer or a gobbler turkey: A good spot is a good spot, and a resident, if removed, will be replaced so that the prime habitat doesn't go unused.

Though Kirby has described the visual aspects of a roosting area, he knows that finding birds can be done by two senses. "You can just go out and do the sight work and locate them by sign, or you can locate them by sound. For a novice hunter or somebody new to an area," Kirby advises, "the best thing to do is simply listen. Get into areas where you've been told turkeys have been. It is natural for a gobbler to gobble. Just prior to the mating season he'll call—you won't have to call at all—and he'll give his position away to you."

THE SHOCK GOBBLE

Kirby says many sounds can make a turkey gobble. "A train whistle or a siren can trigger a gobble," he suggests. "So can a rooster crowing. Depending on the region, it might be a pileated woodpecker, a peacock, a barred owl or a crow. In the West, an elk bugle or coyote howl or horned owl hoot could set him off. These are many of the shrill sounds that might draw a response."

Such a response is called a shock gobble. "That gobbling doesn't necessarily pertain to his mating desire; it's just a reflex, I believe. The bird doesn't really have a chance to think; it just reacts."

Fortunately for the hunter, many of these sounds can be created from calls. The idea is to get the gobbler to sound off so that you can pinpoint his whereabouts. "Even though those sounds that may draw a shock gobble can be emulated by calls, the first call I am going to use no matter where I go is a boat paddle," Kirby admits.

What exactly is a boat paddle? "It's an elongated box call that originated, I believe, in Missouri. They used to be called fencepost calls because hunters made them out of old, broken cedar fenceposts. The original calls were probably 14 or 15 inches long. Because they are longer and slimmer than most box calls, the paddle comes in contact with more of the box. It gives a more diverse sound. First the sound is shrill, then it turns raspy."

"Everybody has a different call that they have the most confidence in. For me, it's the boat paddle," says Kirby. "I'll start off soft and just yelp a little bit. There are soft calls and loud calls, but when I am trying to locate turkeys, I always start off with a soft call. I can always get louder, but if I start off too loud, instead of locating a tom with a gobble I may silence him for quite a while. I have

If the turkeys aren't sounding off, try a shock gobble to get the birds talking a bit, revealing their whereabouts.

so much confidence in the boat paddle," Kirby explains, "that if I don't get a gobble, I don't want to go into that area. There may be a tom there, but if he won't gobble to that call, I'm not going to waste my time on him. I know that some turkeys will come in quietly, but I think the thrill of spring hunting is to hear the bird talking and know he's coming." That's excitement!

No matter what locator call you favor, Kirby's advice is the same: "Drive the roads, stop the car and call. If you've narrowed down to a roosting area, go to it."

Kirby mentioned the various calls that can elicit a gobble and help you locate gobblers.

On roost, when it is still dark or low light, an owl hoot can be particularly effective. So can a coyote howl. Crow calls during the day often draw a gobble. Depending on the part of the country you are in, other creatures' calls can provoke a response.

TURKEY CALLS AS LOCATORS

But sometimes to get a gobble, Kirby will fight fire with fire. "You can locate a gobbler by challenging him. I've got a couple of gobbler calls. When I'm not getting results, I shake them to emit either a boss gobble or challenging jake gobble. I also have a tube call that produces a gobble."

Sometimes, using a gobble to locate a tom won't work by itself. "Throw a hen call in there, then gobble on top of that. The gobbler might not be able to hold himself back. It's like, 'Hey, there's a hen here and there's another gobbler here,' and he's off; it's almost like a shock gobble. He doesn't have time to think about it. His mating instincts take over."

Using a gobbler call, however, does make you out to be a tom turkey, and with any other hunters around, that can put you in a precarious position. "You want to be extremely careful," Kirby warns. "I suggest that you use the gobble primarily early in the morning or early in the evening when you are trying to locate toms on the roost."

PUTTING TURKEYS TO BED

It all comes back to having a good idea of where a bird is roosting. Perhaps the most valuable thing you can do to get a bird as he comes off the roost in the morning is to locate him the evening before, or "put him to bed."

"I may sit along the road just before dusk or I may walk into the area where I suspect the bird might roost, but I don't recommend trying to get any closer than a quarter mile. If I know that somewhere along that ridge over there is likely going to be a turkey going to roost, I'll probably

---

Rise & Shine with Your GPS

What could be more frustrating than putting a big gobbler to bed, dreaming of him all night, getting up hours before dawn to work your way back to his location ... and then losing your way in the dark and missing the fly-down at dawn?

If you hunt familiar country that you know well and your access is limited—such as to a farm or two in the Midwest—you may not have this problem. But what if you're miles from any road in, say, big Ozark timber, a flat expanse of Georgia swamp, a series of Tennessee hollows or an expanse of Wyoming rangeland? Then your salvation could be a hand-held Global Positioning System (GPS) unit.

Simply plot your waypoint—and log it—before you sneak away after putting the turkey to bed. You could even plot a route of several waypoints on your way out if the trek is a long one and the country especially steep. Next morning, navigate your way back in to the roost. Civilian-approved GPS units (the only thing available) might not take you back to the exact tree you were leaning against the evening before, but they'll get you close enough that you'll certainly be able to recognize some landmarks and get situated in time for fly-down.

— Tom Carpenter

sit silently until about 10 minutes before fly-up, which occurs at the end of daylight."

"Then I make some soft calls, though on windy days, when sound doesn't travel as well, I will call more loudly. Often, the tom will gobble before he goes to roost. I just sit and listen to his gobbling on his own, which may occur every three or four minutes. He'll actually help you locate him."

Sometimes the gobbler isn't so cooperative and you have to work a bit harder to find one going on roost. If you're having problems getting gobblers to sound off, Kirby suggests trying an owl call. "Then if nothing happens after about five minutes," he says, "I would make soft yelps. After that, I'd make the sounds hens do before they go on roost: yelps, then cackling and then flying up. Most people don't realize that hens do that fly-up cackle too. They flap their wings and cackle. A lot of times they'll hit a limb, but not quite make it, and cackle some more."

"On dead-calm nights, you can hear the wingbeats, even if you haven't heard any responses to your calls. Adult gobblers are much louder than hens. But if I haven't heard anything—gobbles, wingbeats, nothing—and I'm ready to leave, I'll give some loud yelps. If I don't get a gobble, I'm not going to hunt there in the morning because there probably aren't any turkeys there."

When you've put a bird to bed, however, most of the guesswork of locating the bird the next morning is removed. "Once you've located a turkey on roost, the way you want to get to him in the morning," Kirby advises, "is from above him, rather than from below, if at all possible." Make your approach as quietly and stealthily as possible, so you don't bust the turkey from his roost.

Having problems putting birds to bed? Use an owl call. If that doesn't work, try soft yelps.

Kirby reveals that although the belief that you can't call turkeys downhill is a myth, he does prefer to be at an even keel with his tom come first light.

Then you might want to repeat the drill from the evening before. Use an owl call to see if you can draw a shock gobble, just to assure yourself of his location. Once you've located the gobbler, the rest is in your hands—and mouth. It's time to create a setup and get ready for some action.

Locating turkeys isn't rocket science. But it's hard work—you have to be out there, working, to have your best chance of locating a bird. The time investment is substantial, but it's the best way—maybe the only way—to ensure that you'll at least be close to a turkey when you start hunting the next morning. Listen intently, use locator calls or even turkey calls, mark locations precisely ... and then get to bed so you can rise well before the sun the next morning.

THE RIGHT SETUP

You hear a gobble and now you must decide what to do next. Or perhaps you put birds to roost the evening before and now you have to create and carry out a strategy that will place you in the proper position to take advantage of the tom's location. The scenarios you may run into while turkey hunting are almost endless, but none will end successfully if you don't properly set up to get your bird.

"After hunting all these years," relates Harold Knight, renowned game call manufacturer, television and video host and turkey hunter, "I'd say setting up is probably one of the most important aspects of turkey hunting. The hunter has to pick the right place to set up, and that knowledge comes with experience. He has to mess up a lot before he really knows how to set up. It's a lot of trial and error. The only real shortcut is if you can hunt with an accomplished hunter and learn some of the sport's strategies, techniques and tips."

Harold Knight is just such an accomplished hunter—a shortcut, if you will—and his advice will help you understand the factors and strategies that go into successfully setting up for wild turkeys.

ON THEIR LEVEL

Though you'll do some turkey hunting on flat ground, most of it will be in hilly terrain. That just seems to be the case across a good portion of turkey range. Where, then, should you try to set up on the gobbler you're after?

Knight describes, "I've called turkeys straight up and straight down, but what I like to do most is get on the same elevation that he is. Remember, you want to make his path to you as easy as possible. A difficult path will make him nervous, and he just might decide not to come at all."

"Most of the time I can predict where the gobbler is going to appear. By looking at the terrain and identifying his easiest path—the path that offers the least resistance—you can usually figure where he is going to arrive."

"Another thing to consider regarding setting up when you are hunting ridges, where elevation

About the Expert

Harold Knight killed his first turkey when he was 11 years old, and he's been hunting the birds ever since. His turkey hunting began in Kentucky's Land Between the Lakes area, before the state's restoration program had spread turkeys around the state. At that time, two old-timers took him under their wing, teaching him turkey-hunting techniques that have served him well to this day.

Knight, along with his partner David Hale, founded Knight & Hale Game Calls, a leading manufacturer of game calls, hunting accessories and hunting videotapes. For the last 20 years, Knight figures he has been hunting turkeys with shotgun and video camera 55 to 60 days per season, visiting 10 different states each year. He has hunted turkeys across the continent.

If you can jump across stream or creek, so can a turkey, and that shouldn't stop him. But don't expect to call a tom across a river.

could be a factor, is to avoid the very top. I want to get on the sidehill, not at the crest, because that's the way a gobbler likes to come, not over the top."

AVOID THE BARRIERS

Elevation is a key topographic consideration, but certainly not the only one. "If you can jump across a tiny stream or creek, so can a turkey, and that shouldn't stop him, but don't expect to call a tom across a wider body of water. Once I was filming in Montana when we called a turkey across a river. It landed, strutted and we killed him, but there are very few times that will happen."

"Briar patches can be something they won't want to go through. They like to go where they can see." Artificial barriers can be a problem too, and when setting up, be as familiar with the immediate area you are hunting as possible. "Around agricultural areas, you'll often have woven-wire fences, and you might not know they are there. I once called a turkey for two hours. He

must have gobbled a thousand times. Finally, he just walked off. I couldn't figure out why he wouldn't come in. Finally, I walked down to the area where he had been strutting back and forth and discovered a wire fence. That turkey had come up to the fence and strutted and strutted, waiting for the hen to come up to him, just as it is supposed to happen. Of course, she never did, and he wouldn't cross it. If that fence hadn't been there, the hunt would have been a piece of cake."

PLANNING FOR THE SHOT

When Harold Knight selects a place to set up, elevation and barriers—both topographical and artificial—are on his mind ... and so is his well-being! "I've always got safety on my mind. I try to pick a tree that will cover my whole body. That's in case somebody comes up from behind me and shoots at the bird I am calling, thinking perhaps that I'm a hen that he can't see."

Besides the tree being wide, Knight wants his setup to be at a spot that will allow him a shot as soon as the gobbler becomes visible. "That prevents the turkey from hanging up out at 70 yards, strutting and waiting for the hen to come to him. Say he steps out 70 yards away. That means he can see for 70 yards, and even though he doesn't see the hen, he knows, judging from your calling, that the hen should be able to see him. It's just natural for the hen to come to the gobbler. So he'll try to get into a position for the hen to see him, and that may mean going up to the next level. I want him to be in shotgun range when he comes up over the hill to find the hen."

For the first-time turkey hunter, this is an important point to remember: It is not in a gobbler's instinct to search out a calling hen. The natural way of things is for her to come to him. So when you are calling, remember that trying to get a gobbler to come to you is an unnatural activity for him. So you have to make getting to you as

Moving In

Tom is reluctant to come, so hunter moves carefully in.

Tom struts, nearing fence but not intending to cross it.

While three or four strands of barbed-wire looks open to you, this can be a major obstacle for turkeys. You can slowly low-crawl up closer to the fence and shoot from the prone position. Turkeys have extremely keen eyesight; stay low, move slowly and listen to the gobbling or footsteps to keep informed of the gobbler's location. Stay very alert for other hunters if you move on a gobbler. Here, the hunter realized there is a fence between him and the tom. The hunter crawls carefully closer, then tries to lure the tom closer, into shooting range.

Use the Terrain

Take advantage of the terrain when you set up. Use rises and dips to place yourself strategically so that the turkey will appear within shotgun (or bow) range. In this situation, the hunter could set up at point A, a little closer to the turkey. But a better spot might be at point B, behind the rise. Why? Calling from there could draw the turkey up and over the rise and into immediate range. Calling from spot A might cause the gobbler to hang up in front, out of range, thinking the hen should be able to see him. That gobbler knows exactly where the calling is coming from, and if the source is over a slight rise, he has to work his way over to take a look. Watch closely—you might just get a head peeking over at first—and be prepared!

easy as possible, and that means planning your setup so that he will just appear within shooting range.

TAKING CARE OF DETAILS

Knight likes to carry pruners with him. Their main use is to cut some brush to stick up in front of him to conceal himself partially. "I stick some pieces of brush right in front of me, then test the swing of my shotgun to make sure it clears easily. I also want to make sure that any other obstacles are far enough away not to interfere with a shot, even if I have to move to my right or my left. That little bit of brush just breaks up my shape a little more and makes me a bit blurrier to the turkey." A second use of the pruners is to clear a shooting path if necessary.

A seat or a cushion contributes to comfort. "Most of the time I am sitting on something between me and the ground. When you are comfortable you are a better sitter. If you are not comfortable, whether you realize it or not, you move a lot. I always carry a cushion. But I've used all kinds of seats. For instance, the National Wild Turkey Federation sells a portable stool that has legs higher on one side than the other. So, if I'm on the side of one of those hills, backed up against a tree, I can level myself with that stool." The bottom line is that no matter what you use, make sure it is camouflaged and comfortable. You absolutely have to be able to sit still for long, intense periods without fidgeting.

When Knight selects his spot to set up, he wants to make sure that there aren't a lot of low limbs and blowdowns between him and the spot where he thinks the gobbler might first appear. "That tom is going to walk around them. He's going to walk where he can see."

After Knight has selected his spot, he settles in by squaring himself to where he thinks the gobbler will appear. He also places his gun on his knee, pointing toward that same spot. "I never lay down my gun. When I sit down to call the turkey, I have my gun up and ready. When a turkey is hidden, you can maybe move slightly, even make noise with leaves. But when he comes into view and into range and you move, the party's over. So move when the terrain blocks him, but do your best to have your gun ready." In addition, you never know when that turkey will appear, or how close he really is. One cluck and he might be in range. So be ready to shoot from the start!

"When the turkey approaches, most people expect him to walk right into view, exposing his

A two-person setup will place the caller behind the shooter. Get comfortable before you go to work, to minimize your fidgeting. A decoy or a real hen—if you are fortunate enough to attract one—might help bring the gobbler into range.

whole body. But most of the time, he will put his head up like a periscope. He'll turn his head, look and walk a bit. Then he'll do it again, craning his head, looking, then walking. He hardly ever just walks straight toward you. That head may be all the hunter sees for a while. A person's got to be ready to shoot that turkey as soon as he sees a visible beard and knows it's a legal turkey."

BLINDS AND DECOYS

Knight sometimes makes blinds more elaborate than brush stuck in the ground a few feet in front of him. "I make blinds more often in the fall, when I've broken up a flock and I know the birds are going to come back to reassemble. Also, in the spring, in states where I can hunt in the afternoon, I might know of a field or other area where gobblers strut. I will then craft a makeshift blind out of camouflage material or sticks and brush, creating a spot where I can sit comfortably. Then I'll put out a decoy and call every now and then. The first thing you know, you hear an old turkey gobbling, then you see him strutting, and next he's by that decoy."

Knight likes to use decoys in his setup, though he does think they have their limitations. "I do not like to use a decoy in heavily wooded situations but I love to put a decoy in an open place, like a logging road. This may on occasion spook the birds, but the tactic works often enough that it is worth trying. I put the decoys out within shotgun range, maybe 30 to 35 yards, somewhere the approaching turkey will be able to see it."

The Kentuckian cautions that once a turkey sees the decoy, he'll stop gobbling. So, if things get quiet all of the sudden and you can't see the gobbler, listen for the drumming, spitting sound that often accompanies his strutting.

When Knight is setting out a single decoy, it is a hen. At times, however, he'll use two decoys. "I'll use a jake and a hen decoy. I'll put them 10 to 15 yards apart, placing the jake where I want my gobbler to come. The gobbler, most of the time, will come to that male decoy. He may try to pluck it or kick it or fight it, but if the tom comes that close to the decoy, he's in trouble."

CREATING THE SETUP: ROOSTING TURKEYS

Many hunters put in a lot of effort trying to locate birds the evening before the hunt, attempting to pinpoint their roosting sites. That gobbler is often roosted near some hens that he would like to hook up with in the morning. In a situation like this, the setup is an essential ingredient in the strategy to bring the gobbler to your call.

"When a gobbler is roosting near hens, you have a situation that could be good—or it could

Though there are as many decoy strategies as there are hunters, one rule you should always follow is to place the decoys within shooting range. That gobbler might come right in.

be bad," says Knight. "If you can get between where the hens are roosted and where the gobbler is roosted, you've got a great setup. Unfortunately, you can't do that a lot of times because you'll scare a turkey. If you spook your tom, you've blown it, at least for a couple of hours; but if you simply scare a hen, that's fine."

"I don't mind scaring hens off the roost near daylight. When the tom hears them flying, he'll gobble. When things have settled down a while, I'll flap my hat against my body to imitate the sound of a flying turkey and give a fly-down cackle. Then I'll give some yelps, and the next thing I know he's sailing off his roost and is right on top of me."

Knight summarizes his strategies for getting in close to the turkeys—before creating the setup—as follows: "I'm always trying to get between the gobbler and the hens. If the hens fly down and start walking toward the gobbler's location, I'll do something to try to scare the hens off if I can. On the other hand, if I hear the hens calling and the gobbler answering them, I will head toward the hens, because that's where he's going. I don't care how well you call—you could be 10 times world champion—it's difficult to impossible to outcall a real turkey."

CREATING THE SETUP: MORE STRATEGIES

The most exciting turkey-hunting scenario involves a hunter setting up after he has heard a gobble. Sometimes, however, hours of hunting may not produce a gobble or a hen cluck—at this point, a study of turkey patterns may suggest a strategy to use.

Though Harold Knight prefers to walk and call, walk and call, always listening for a response from a tom, he knows there are times when just sitting down can be a good setup. Yes, you can do this even if you haven't heard a gobble.

"If I am in the woods, I may set up on one side of a saddle, just below where I know birds feed. I'll listen for that clucking and scratching, and hopefully I can call one so that when he comes up over the saddle, he'll be in shotgun range."

When a hunter moves and calls—and gets a gobbler to respond—it's time to determine the best place to set up.

"Another situation in which I'll simply set up, even if I haven't heard or seen a gobbler, is when the birds are nesting. Then I know the birds will be around the fields, morning and afternoon, and that's where I will be. A lot of times I will set up on those wooded points that extend out into the fields. I've killed a lot of turkeys that way."

Knight believes that hunting with a companion greatly improves your odds of your scoring. "The hunter with the gun should set up in a good spot, and the one who isn't planning on shooting should set up 50 to 75 yards behind him and do the calling. It's unreal what you can do, especially on turkeys that are used to hanging up." The idea, of course, is that the gobbler moves toward the caller, coming in range of the shooter before the

Hunting with a Partner: Two Strategies

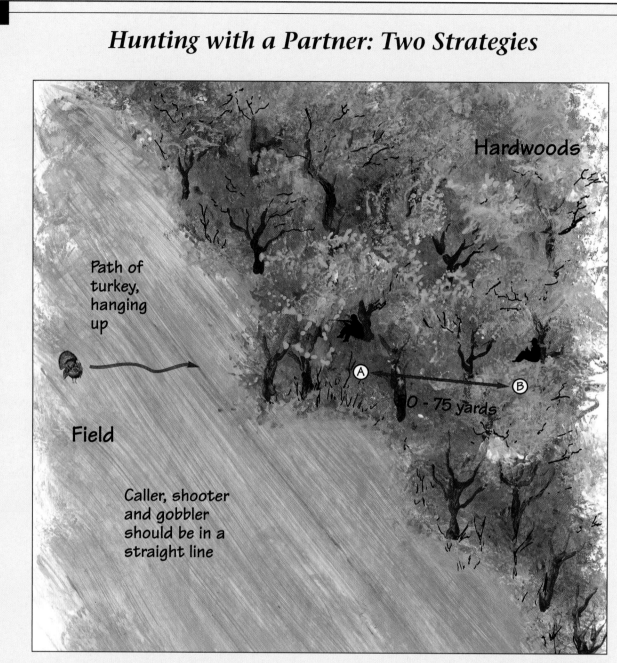

Hardwoods

Path of
turkey,
hanging
up

Field

Caller, shooter
and gobbler
should be in a
straight line

(A) 0 - 75 yards (B)

SHOOTER AHEAD OF CALLER

In this setup, the shooter (A) sets up on a straight line between the turkey and the caller. The caller (B) does his or her work from 50 to 75 yards behind the shooter. This is a good situation because an approaching gobbler will be focused in on the calling and its location, rather than on where a shooter might be. In addition, tom turkeys have a maddening tendency to hang up 50 to 75 yards from the source of the calling; this plan puts the shooter right in that area. The caller should be prepared as well, in case the target turkey somehow sneaks around the shooter—or another turkey silently slips in to the calling from another direction. If both hunters plan to shoot, partners must agree on shooting safety rules in advance.

HUNTING BACK-TO-BACK

Here, both hunters sit at-the-ready, back-to-back against a large tree. In this setup, the strategic spot is a point of woods jutting into a hayfield. One hunter calls and has his or her gun ready; the other remains ready to shoot. Turkeys like to circle, so one hunter or the other should be in position for a good shot. Because both potential routes are covered, neither hunter has to shift much, if at all, to aim and make the shot ... which means less chance of spooking the bird. Because the hunters are back-to-back, safety considerations are taken care of.

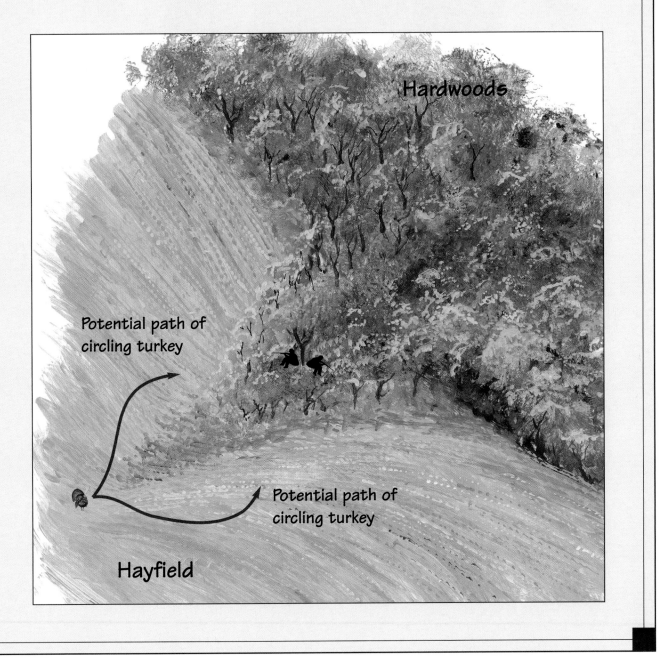

Hardwoods

Potential path of circling turkey

Potential path of circling turkey

Hayfield

There are many ways to improve your success by hunting with a partner. A chief benefit: One hunter can call while the other concentrates on shooting. Movement is minimized, increasing the odds that the gobblers won't detect your setup.

tom gets close enough to the calling to become suspicious.

Sometimes, of course, both hunters will want a crack at the shooting action. "Then hunters should sit right next to each other or a few yards apart. Agree with your partner beforehand: You shoot a bird on the left, I'll shoot one on the right, or whatever makes sense. In fact, it makes sense to face opposite directions because a turkey's nature is often to circle." For instance, sit with your backs against the same tree, guns facing different directions.

The best advice that Harold Knight offers to both solo hunters or paired-up hunters is to have lots of different strategies in mind for setting up— and be flexible. "You cannot have your 'speech' written before you go. If you do, the birds will force you to change it every time, because there are so many variables in turkey hunting. That's the reason I like turkey hunting so much. Those birds will humble me, and I don't care how good you are. If you go turkey hunting often enough, they'll humble you."

Knight is right. But if you pay attention to his advice on setting up, you'll find yourself eating turkey breast every now and then … a nice break from humble pie.

Moving on Birds

"You Yankees are supposed to be fast-paced and aggressive," Steve Barras told me, "and we Southerners are supposed to be slow-paced and laid-back. But when it comes to turkey hunting, you and I seem to be just the opposite."

An Aggressive Hunt

Barras made that summation to me after an early-morning turkey hunt in the hills of New York's Hudson Valley, where I live and do a lot

Hunting Strategies, Techniques & Tactics

Turkeys, according to Steve Barras, are always on the move. A hunter has to make himself aggressive by seeking opportunities to simulate the traveling nature of wild turkeys, while at the same time concealing himself.

About the Expert

*S*teve Barras has successfully hunted turkeys throughout the U.S., tagging birds in 30 states. Barras is a wildlife biologist who has combined his skills in wildlife biology and economics to enjoy a successful career as both a wildlife manager and chief financial officer.

Though Barras's roots are in the South—he grew up in Alabama, lives in Georgia and spends much of his working time in Florida—his aggressive style of hunting wild turkeys does not fit into what many of us believe is the laid-back Southern approach to life.

of turkey hunting. I'm still not 100 percent comfortable with the strategy he displayed, but I can't contest the fact that it worked.

The morning had begun typically enough. As the sun was first beginning to show signs of making an appearance, a gobbler, perhaps across the road that bisected this steep hollow, sounded off. He was hundreds of yards away, on a piece of posted property to which we did not have access.

Barras was not discouraged. He yelped and cut with his diaphragm caller—and the gobbler responded. Barras picked up the cadence of his calling to a feverish crescendo, and the gobbler—now maybe two—seemed to answer with similar urgency.

We set up 100 yards east of a power line that climbed to the mountain's crest, and we were in the midst of a beautiful, open hardwood forest. Grassy woods lanes, a heap of discarded medicine, milk and liquor bottles, and perpendicular stone walls provided the only evidence that the area was once a farm.

The birds—it now sounded like there was certainly more than one—had seemed an impossible distance away before, but now responded from low in the hollow. I couldn't tell whether they had crossed over to our side of the road. While they moved toward us, gobbling in response to Barras's calls, I was content to stay put. Not Barras.

MOVING IN

Staying low, he headed downhill in the gobblers' general direction. His tactic surprised me, but I got up and mimicked his stealthy approach. I quickly realized that I wasn't there to guide my Southern guest; I was merely the means of access to this piece of property. Barras was doing the calling, and he was dictating the strategy!

The gobblers seemed closer with each response, but Barras continued to call and move, sometimes to the left, sometimes to the right. At one point, I said to myself, "Enough. If he wants to try to move on birds, let him."

I wasn't going to take the chance of my 6-foot-3-inch frame, not as inconspicuous as Barras's smaller and more wiry body, blowing our cover and my guest's chance at his first New York turkey. I also didn't feel comfortable "stalking" these birds. It went against the rules of safety I had known since my early days of turkey hunting. From that point on, he was on his own.

At first, I could hear his excited calling and the response from what now seemed to be a mountainside of gobblers. What began as a single tom gobbling hundreds of yards away became a

Aggressive turkey hunting may arouse gobblers so much, they might fight with each other for the right to romance the hen that you are pretending to be. By hunting aggressively, you may bring out the aggressive nature of the bird you are after.

choir. I suddenly heard a shot, and a few minutes later Barras came into sight—empty-handed.

"I snuck up to a stone wall and set up there," he described as fast as an excited Southerner can, still grimacing after missing his gobbler. "When I peeked over the wall, I must have seen 15 males and the few females they were following," he said breathlessly. "They were excited. They all wanted me, or at least the hen that I tried to be by calling and moving frequently. Four big gobblers were fighting over me. Two at a time, their necks were twisted around one another, and they were pecking away at each other. Every now and then one of the onlooking jakes would sneak in and do some backbiting."

"That went on, almost in rounds," he said, then paused. "The kill would have been anticlimactic. Seeing that display was the highlight of the hunt."

His honesty seemed genuine, rather than a rationalization from wounded pride. The highlight for me was watching a hunting technique very different from the spring tactics I regularly practiced. With the birds coming in, I would have been content to stay put.

STRATEGIES FOR MOVING ON TURKEYS

"The only turkey that stays put is a hen on a nest," Barras explains. "Otherwise, turkeys are on the move, feeding or looking for company. Even turkeys on the roost may move from limb to limb. A hunter has to make himself aggressive and seek opportunities to simulate birds while still concealing himself. I'm not bushwhacking the birds—I'm just upping my chances of getting them to come to me."

As educated as Barras is about turkeys and turkey behavior, he

Moving In - A Case Study

A wild turkey might respond to a call but then hesitate to come in all the way. Here, the gobbler came as far as a stone wall but hesitated to come over it. The hunter sneaked along a perpendicular stone wall, on the opposite side from the tom, to conceal his own approach while getting into range of a shot. Barras's method takes advantage of topographical features to offer trails and concealment for his movement.

admits that his introduction to aggressive turkey hunting came completely by accident.

"For a couple of years I'd been working a big gobbler that always seemed to hang up 75 to 100 yards away," Barras recalls. "Out of frustration, I simply gave up on the gobbler and started to walk away, continuing to call in hopes of locating another tom."

"Well, wouldn't you know it, the gobbler that I had been calling must have gotten upset about the prospect of losing me to another tom and sounded off with double and triple gobbles while on the run toward me—much closer than he had been when I was set up."

The stubborn gobbler was soon in Barras's vest, and since then, Barras has applied that knowledge and experience to develop his aggressive turkey-hunting technique.

"I study topographical features to find concealment and trails for my movement," he discloses. "River- and creekbottoms, hills, mountains, ridges, thickets and other features become prime targets. In New York, I used the stone walls."

On one occasion, Barras used a creekbed as his path to a particularly resistant gobbler that had stymied him for three years. Instead of moving toward the bird, Barras played hard to get, moving away from the gobbler. Using the creekbed for cover, Barras quietly backtracked, discreetly set up and greeted the big tom with a volley of number 6s.

"When the birds act excited, I do too. It contributes to their fervor and hastens their approach. When the birds are reluctant, I may call sparingly as well. I don't want the bird waiting on me to come to him. I want him moving to me."

Not only does the amount of calling affect the birds' behavior, but so does the type of calling, Barras explains. "Sometimes I'll call with two dif-

Study topographical features to find concealment and trails for your movement. River- and creekbottoms, hills, mountains, ridges, thickets, stone walls and fences are such possibilities.

ferent calls. The variety of calls excites them. Sometimes I'll cut; sometimes I'll mimic a combination of purrs and cuts that is hard to describe in words, but one that I've often heard in the woods."

"When the tom sounds excited," he repeats, leaning forward, "so do I."

Barras also varies his calls from high to low pitches and adds decoys every now and then to help set the stage.

"Singing the scale is music to their ears," he remarks, smiling, "but decoys limit your mobility. They help in arousing the tom's jealous and aggressive tendencies, but at the same time, you want to be able to move quickly and be

Moving In—Stream as Barrier

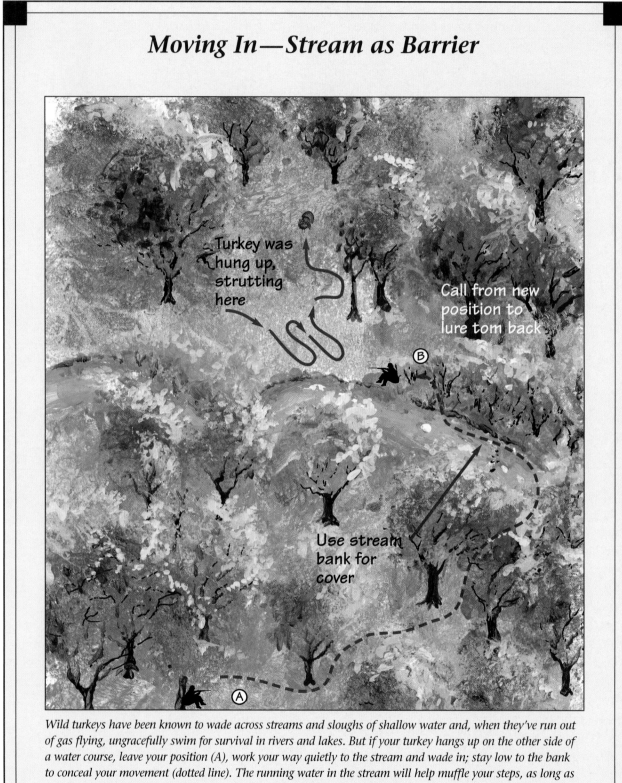

Turkey was hung up, strutting here

Call from new position to lure tom back

B

Use stream bank for cover

A

Wild turkeys have been known to wade across streams and sloughs of shallow water and, when they've run out of gas flying, ungracefully swim for survival in rivers and lakes. But if your turkey hangs up on the other side of a water course, leave your position (A), work your way quietly to the stream and wade in; stay low to the bank to conceal your movement (dotted line). The running water in the stream will help muffle your steps, as long as you do not move large rocks against each other. If the creekbottom becomes too slippery to walk in safely, stop and unload your shotgun; no turkey is worth risking your life for. By now the bird will have walked away, so slip up near to where he was strutting (B) and begin calling softly. Don't be afraid to move on a turkey, but do stay alert to your surroundings!

Moving Back—Edge of Woods as Barrier

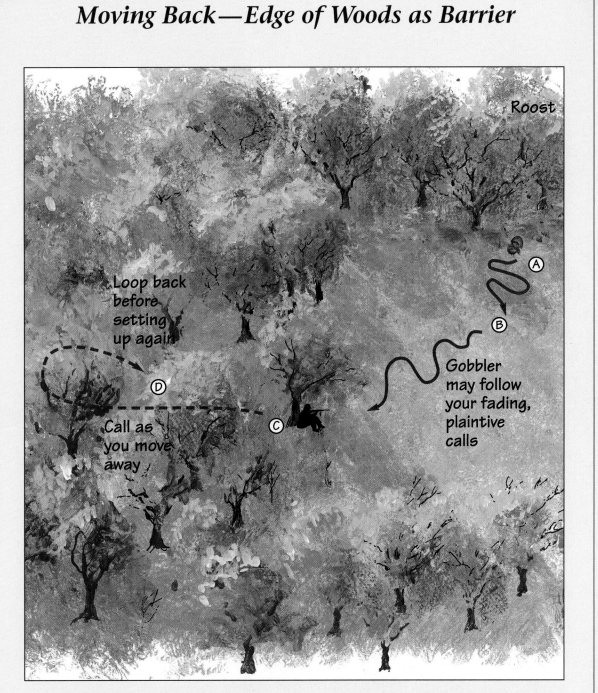

Roost

Loop back before setting up again

Call as you move away

Gobbler may follow your fading, plaintive calls

Turkeys tend to fly from the roost to an open area. As wary birds, they like to stay in the open where they have greater visibility. Nature dictates that a hen goes to the gobbler. If you move and call while going away from the gobbler, quietly move back near your first location and stay alert. A turkey may sound like a human slowly walking through the woods. You might also hear drumming!

Here, a gobbler has (A) landed safely in an open hay field after a night on roost. He struts in the field (B) but won't approach the woodline as the hunter calls. The hunter leaves his original position (C), calling as he moves away and then looping back (D) to watch his backtrail, where the tom may follow.

Hunting Strategies, Techniques & Tactics

A gobbler that will display for your calling well out of range is a perfect subject for a more aggressive type of approach. Sneak closer to the bird or, perhaps, move away as you call—to increase his aggression and possibly spur him to move.

concealed. Sometimes taking the time to retrieve your decoy can be the deterrent in attracting a hot gobbler that you didn't realize was in viewing distance of your decoy."

The main precaution relating to Barras's aggressive turkey hunting concerns safety. That, of course, is the primary consideration of any turkey hunt.

"I prefer to do this kind of hunting on private land, or on public land where I know hunting pressure is light," Barras admits. "Most importantly, you must keep an eye out not only for where you think the turkey is, but where you are going. In the South, for instance, a big rattler or cottonmouth could be under your next step." Keeping your eyes open for other hunters is just as important.

"Aggressive turkey hunting may not be for everybody," Barras acknowledges, "but there's no denying that it is effective." I know. I've seen it in action.

TAKING WEATHER
INTO ACCOUNT

Come snow, rain, cold, heat, fog or winds, the turkeys are out there. The only way to get one is to just go out and hunt.

*I*f you ask noted hunting personality Ray Eye when the best time to go turkey hunting is, he'll tell you, "When it's turkey season!" In other words, turkey seasons aren't long enough for a hunter to be choosy. "The birds are out there 365 days a year, no matter what the weather. If a hunter is going to get them, he'd better be out there too."

This is especially true considering the way some state game agencies conduct turkey hunts. In those states, when you draw a license, you have one specific window, say a few days to a week, in which to hunt. This is good because it spreads out hunting pressure and gives more hunters the

opportunity to pursue turkeys. But it also means you might not have the luxury of waiting for a picture-perfect turkey-hunting day. You've got to hunt when your license says you can.

But if Eye had to choose ideal conditions for turkey hunting in the spring, this is what he would order: "Cool temperatures, slightly overcast skies and no wind. The birds seem to gobble more on those types of mornings, even more so than on bluebird mornings."

As any turkey hunter knows, ideal conditions like that prevail sometimes, but not always. Although Eye believes that the turkeys generally frequent the same areas in any weather condition—with wind being the exception—he knows that a turkey hunter has to make certain adjustments when adverse weather moves in.

When the other elements of weather come into play, Eye factors them into his hunting strategy. Here are his insights, gleaned from more than three decades of hunting experience.

WIND

"Wind makes it difficult to hear the gobblers, and it makes it difficult for them to hear you. I also think turkeys are more wary in the wind because they can't hear well. They're always alert, always looking and they are more afraid of danger because one of their key senses has been impaired. They will be jumpy, rattled by blowing limbs and things moving around them."

So Eye first looks for the areas to which turkeys may retreat to feel more comfortable. "Of course, it depends on the type of terrain you are hunting. In northern Missouri, for instance, we have rolling hills between which are what we call 'ditches.' I will hunt those ditches. I try to get off the hilltops and go down to the hillsides and into those valleys. The turkeys will do their best to get out of the wind, so I do too." This is good advice in any turkey country where terrain is uneven. No matter where the wind is coming from, there's usually a place to escape it.

Eye takes advantage of the wind to carry the sound of his calls. "I try to set up where the wind can carry the sound of my calls in the direction I think the turkeys are."

With that in mind, he uses calls that will be carried by the wind. "I'll go to a loud box call," he reveals. "I'll also use a heavier latex mouth call, but I use the box call almost exclusively on windy days. If I can't find an area sheltered from the wind, I'll set up where I think the birds may be, judging from hunting on calm days. I'll set up and call for an hour in one spot. Then I may move only 100 or 200 yards, depending on how hard the wind is blowing, and set up again. The harder the wind is blowing, the more difficult it is for the turkeys and me to hear, so the distance between one setup to the next will be shorter. That's how I'll cover my hunting area."

In windy conditions, Eye advises, "You have to use your eyes more than your ears because turkeys may come in and you won't even hear them." That statement reveals one of the advantages of hunting in windy weather—since turkeys can't hear you as well, you can get closer to them.

RAIN

"Of course, it's dangerous to go out hunting in a lightning storm or when other severe weather—like a tornado—is likely. But if the turkey season is open and you want to fill your tag, you have to hunt hard for every available minute when the

Hunting the Wind

When the wind is blowing hard, the best plan of action is to get out of it. In this instance, the hunters have elected to set up in the bottom of a hollow (in some places it might be called a coulee or a canyon), along a field or meadow edge. This spot is protected from the wind, which is roaring over the top but relatively mellow down where the hunters sit. The turkeys know this, too, and should be in the vicinity. Here, the hunters have set up back-to-back against a tree on the leeward side of the hollow; this setup will also take advantage of any breeze that is moving, carrying the sounds of calling across the valley, as well as penetrating the cover nearby.

Rain can work as a turkey hunter's benefit, keeping down the competition, for one thing. Don't forget to protect your box calls and wear good raingear for comfort and, ultimately, for the ability to stay out there and stay still.

conditions are maybe miserable but not life-threatening. For instance, you've got to hunt when it's just raining; I've bagged a lot of turkeys in the rain. A benefit of hunting in the wet woods is that you usually have the area all to yourself."

"I'll move and call, just like I do in the wind, but I'll cover more distance between calling sessions because my calls will be traveling farther. If you are hunting country that has field edges—open pastures and crop fields—work them in a hard rain."

"If it's just a steady, light rain, I'll go to where I have scouted and heard gobblers on clear days. I won't set up for as long a time as I would on windy days. For one thing, my calls will be carrying farther. For another, I'll have the woods to myself, so I don't have to worry as much about running into other hunters. I'll go from one favorite spot to the next, moving and calling. I'll use both my box call and my mouth call, and I'll usually do some aggressive cutting with the diaphragm and real loud yelping on the box call."

In inclement weather, Eye takes extra measures to keep his box call dry. "I'm very careful about how I use it. I'll keep it in a plastic bag in an inside pocket. I can even call with it while it is in the bag. I keep it chalked well, and sometimes I'll take rosin, the same rosin you'd use on violin strings, and I'll coat the lid of my box with it. Then it is less likely that the water will negatively affect it or the sound it produces."

Of course, besides protecting your gear, you have to protect yourself from the rain. "In my vest I carry an excellent-quality rain suit that repels the rain and keeps out the breeze, and I always have a cushion to sit on. A good tip is to carry a couple of dark-green plastic garbage bags in your vest all the time. Use one to sit on. On the other you can cut armholes and a head hole and create an alternative to raingear, which can often be very scratchy and noisy. Just take off your camo shirt or jacket, slip on the garbage bag, then put the outerwear over it. That way you will stay dry and your outfit will still be relatively quiet in the woods."

COLD

"Dress warmly, because if you are not comfortable, you aren't going to be effective and you're not going to have fun. I layer my clothing, starting off with long underwear and heavy pants and shirt and then a jacket. If it gets warmer, I can always pull something off and stow it. That's one reason for wearing a turkey vest with a big pouch in the back."

Though a drop in temperature may affect how many layers of clothes you wear—and how active the turkeys are—it shouldn't affect your turkey-hunting strategy.

"If, all of a sudden, we get a cold snap, that may subdue the gobbling, but you can't judge an area on the amount of gobbling you hear. If you've scouted and you know gobblers are in the area, they'll still be there in the cold. So you've got to do the same thing you'd do otherwise—move and call, move and call, move and call. I've called in spring gobblers when the thermometer read 30°F."

SNOW

"I really haven't seen much effect on the birds because of snow. We've had snow on opening day right here in Missouri. Our group killed three big gobblers while snowflakes as big as silver dollars were coming down. Despite the heavy snow, the birds gobbled and came in. If fact, you could see them very well because of their contrast to the white background."

"Another time we were in the Black Hills of South Dakota. The snow was blowing so hard and the wind was howling—you could almost call it a blizzard. But I went out, getting off the top of the hills into those big hollows. I moved and called, moved and called and

A cold snap might subdue the gobbling, but you can't give up. Dress warmly and keep moving and calling, moving and calling.

Snow might be cold and wet, but the birds are out in it, and if you aren't, you are not going to get your gobbler.

finally started a gobbler. He came in and I shot him. There were 20 people in our camp. Eighteen of them stayed at camp. The owner of the place and I were the only ones who went out, and we each got a bird."

"It goes back to the same point: You've got to be out there. If it's snowing and you stay in camp, you are not going to shoot a turkey." There's just no way you're going to shoot a turkey while sitting on your couch, in your truck or at camp.

An important aspect of hunting in the snow is taking advantage of the sign it may show. Look for the larger gobbler tracks, for straight lines made by the dragged wings of a strutting gobbler, for feathers and for places where the turkeys have scratched through the snow for food. The depth of the snow might affect the birds' choice of feeding grounds.

"If there is a ton of snow, like there was in Missouri a few years ago when we got 26 inches the week before the opener, the birds head for

Extreme heat is a horrid condition to hunt in. Yet, because the birds may be less active in very hot weather, you must become even more active, covering a lot of ground while calling until you come upon that one gobbler that chooses to respond to you.

the thickets, cedar trees and other places that offer cover to them and their food supplies. But when there is just a few inches, especially in areas where the turkeys are used to living through a lot of snow in the winter, they'll be right out in it, working and scratching away in their usual feeding spots."

Eye adds some advice on personal comfort. "Combine the tips on how to dress in cold and rainy weather," he says. "If you can't stay warm and dry, you can't be comfortable. And if you are miserable, it is hard to be an effective turkey hunter." In other words, take good care of yourself. If you're not feeling good and don't feel like hunting, then you're unlikely to be out there working hard for your bird.

EXTREME HEAT

"Extreme heat is a horrible condition to hunt in, but if that's what you're faced with, so be it. You've got to hunt. I try to take advantage of early daylight. Turkey activity seems to decline a bit during the middle of the day, especially when it is

unbearably hot. States like Texas, Oklahoma and Kansas, which allow hunting all day, can really get torrid in midday."

"It seems, the birds just take a midday siesta. They loaf around and will seek shade under trees. I've seen them in Texas then, down in the canyons, seeking some cooler, shady spots the canyon walls offer. They may be less active, but that means you should be more active."

"You'll have to move more and work harder to find birds. There may be a lot of birds that are not receptive to your calling, but someplace out there is one that will respond. So you just have to move and call, move and call. You never know. If you don't give up, the next ridge, the next hill or the next canyon might be the one holding a bird that will gobble to your calls."

Of course, you have to pace yourself, rest on occasion, wear light clothing and prevent dehydration. "I always carry cool drinks. What I like to do is keep a lot of those drinks that come in soft boxes or pouches in the freezer until I'm ready to go hunting. Then I'll throw them in my pack. I may do the same thing with sandwiches. They'll thaw fairly quickly in the extreme heat, and I'll have refreshingly cool beverages and food when I can really appreciate them."

Fog

"It's almost eerie when a gobbler comes out of the fog and becomes visible. He looks like a ghost. Really thick fog can be tough to hunt in, but it shouldn't affect your success," says Eye.

"What you really have to take into consideration is safety because of the tough visibility. You have to be extremely careful in areas where there are other hunters. Be more sensitive than ever to the safety aspects of turkey hunting, especially so far as identifying your target. Don't let hearing an approaching bird replace the need for a definite visual identification."

"Actually, sometimes fog can be an ally to the hunter," Eye points out. "I've started gobblers in the fog, and I was able to get a better position on the birds and set up somewhat closer than I normally would." The fog adds another form of cover for you. In addition, fog seems to improve calling range, if for no other reason than foggy conditions usually equate with calm conditions.

Weather as an Ally

If weather seems to shut down the gobblers, you can counter with a strategy that often works. "Learn the gobbler yelp. Take a box, slate or mouth call, slow your rhythm down and lengthen your yelp. Give off clucks and cuts that are coarser than usual in an area where you know gobblers have been. The gobblers have a pecking order, and if a tom has a particular territory and he thinks another gobbler has moved in, he may come in to fight."

"Or, if it is early in the season, the gobblers might still be hanging together. But they might have been scattered, say by a hunter, so by yelping like a gobbler you may be calling another one in to reassemble. He'll come in yelping and cutting."

The bottom line? "If you are not out there hunting," Eye reemphasizes, "you are not going to hear and find turkeys." It's that simple. If you ask one of our country's top turkey hunters—Ray Eye—weather is almost never an acceptable reason to stay at home or lounge in camp. The gobblers don't do that; they're right out where they always were. You can get them!

Fog can be an ally to a hunter because you may be able to set up closer to the responding gobbler than clear weather would allow.

FALL HUNTING

In the spring season, you are taking advantage of the wild turkey's mating instincts to entice the gobbler to come to you. In the fall, when male and female turkeys are legal game in the states that hold autumn seasons, you can't use the breeding desire to your advantage. But according to Bill Hollister, you can capitalize on other aspects of a turkey's social behavior.

Hollister typically fills the two-bird limit in his homestate of New York each fall, and he often does it by tagging adult gobblers, a particularly tough challenge. "Wild turkeys are very gregarious, very social," he remarks. "Adult hens in the fall may gather with one, two, maybe even three other adult hens and their young of the year. If they are not gathered with those other flocks, they at least know the other groups in the area and recognize them by their calling. Usually, gobblers of the same age band together too."

LOCATING AUTUMN BIRDS

So, in the autumn, birds aren't dispersed here and there about their habitat. Rather, they're grouped up ... harder to find because there are not birds in every corner of the woods; they're concentrated.

"The challenge then becomes finding the birds,

and you'll do that by looking for sign," says Hollister. "You'll also spend a lot of time just walking, looking for birds." Among the sign that Hollister scouts for is scratching—telltale turned-over leaves and raked soil indicating that birds have been searching for food. "Look along water courses—small creeks and intermittent streams—where food is often concentrated," he advises. This is because the extra moisture makes for better plants and increased insect density. "Also, in late summer and early fall, check out grassy fields, because turkeys love to feed on grasshoppers."

Finding the turkeys' food supply can definitely lead you to turkeys in the fall, but because of their wide selection of food sources, locating concentrated feeding areas may be a challenge. "They'll turn from insects to soft mast—gray dogwood berries, wild grapes, black cherries and chokecher-

Gray dogwood is a soft mast turkeys favor in the fall.

ries, thorn apples, winter berries, buckthorn, barberry and the like. Then they'll go to the hard mast—red and white oak acorns, hickory and beech nuts— which will last them through the winter. Where there are dairy farms, undigested food in the spread cow manure can sustain the birds through a tough winter." Even harvested grain fields can draw turkeys in for feeding.

Locate the food supply—such as acorns—and you'll find birds.

"These are just examples of their food supply; turkeys have been known to eat more than 400 varieties of food, including the innards of dead deer. They may, in truth, have the most diverse appetite of any animal."

SCATTERING STRATEGIES

Because calling undisturbed birds to the hunter is a tactic that is not as dependable in the fall as in the spring, when the mating urge is at its height, a hunter must employ a different strategy. "The major technique is to find the birds and scatter them," explains Hollister. "Then take advan-

If birds fly far in the same direction, little has been achieved. Your goal: Get them to scatter in many directions.

tage of their desire to reassemble by locating yourself strategically and using the correct calls."

Before you can get to the point of scattering the flock, however, you must locate the birds. As mentioned, knowing their food sources is obviously a great lead. But according to Hollister, putting on some mileage through stealthy walking can find the birds before they find you. "Using the contours of the topography you are hunting will allow you to approach the birds closely enough to get a good scatter or even to get a bird before the breakup."

"Safety is always a concern, but stalking and sneaking is not the danger in the fall that it is in the spring, when you may be stalking a calling bird or a hunter."

Getting close is a key to getting a good scatter. "I've talked to hunters who complain that every time they try to scatter birds by charging and screaming, the birds simply run off all in the same direction. They don't really disperse the birds. I ask them, 'Did you shoot over the birds' heads?' They always say no. If you shoot just one time above the birds, they'll usually scatter."

"The best scatter is when you get almost all the birds airborne. If some run off, that's okay, as long as others fly or run off in opposite directions. Getting them scattered in all different directions—360 degrees—doesn't often happen."

SETTING UP

Once the birds have scattered, you must figure out where to locate yourself and know what calls to use. If you can scatter the birds in many different directions, chances are the birds—especially hens and poults—will attempt to reassemble close to the point where they were initially dispersed.

"If the birds scattered by fanning out, sometimes they'll get together at an assembly point in the direction that they all flew. Then they may get together very soon," says Hollister. "If you scatter adult gobblers, they'll usually reassemble by approaching the scatter point from a higher elevation. They will come in from a point where they can observe the area from which they were scattered. So it's often advantageous to go a little bit higher on the ridge from where you scattered them—you may get the birds coming right to you."

In any case, Hollister will constructively use the time before the birds start to reassemble, which could be a few minutes (early in the season) or 45 minutes (later in the season when the birds already may have been scattered on other occasions). Adult gobblers might take hours to

These hunters took advantage of the birds' desire to regroup.

Hunting in Fall: The Scatter

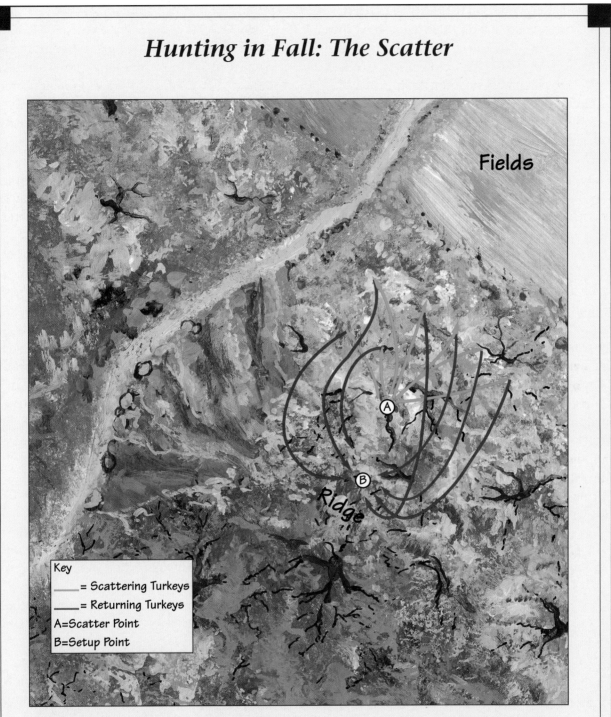

Fields

Key

___ = Scattering Turkeys
___ = Returning Turkeys
A=Scatter Point
B=Setup Point

Ridge

In fall, the hunting strategies are a little different than in spring, but you still have to call the birds. In this situation, the hunter scatters the turkeys at point A, hoping to get them flying off in different directions; you want this so that the birds have to call and move around to regroup into their flock. The hunter then has two options: setting up near the point where the scatter occurred, or heading uphill 50 to 100 yards to a strategic setup spot to start calling the birds back (B). Why set up uphill from the scatter point? Because often turkeys, especially wary adult toms, will circle around and uphill, trying to come from above and descend on the scatter point as they re-group—possibly in an attempt to see if the danger that flushed them is still there. And, your calls will project further if you're higher in elevation.

reassemble. Hollister will use the time to select a comfortable setup that could present a good shot. He'll even cut small leafy branches and stick them in the ground around the tree he has chosen to sit by, creating a blind to help conceal himself.

Once he has settled in, he waits for the calling to begin. "If you are dealing with hens and poults, you will be using assembly yelps and kee-kee runs—the high-pitched whistling of an attempted yelp of immature birds—to get the birds to come to you. With adult gobblers, you'll use mainly coarse clucks and yelps at a slower cadence than hens would use."

Sometimes the flocks will not have such distinct divisions. "Often, late in the season—especially if you have snow on the ground—you may get mixed flocks of adult gobblers with hens and poults. When you break up a mixed flock, the hens and poults will usually reassemble first. But a couple of years ago, we had just the opposite occur when the very first bird to come in was an adult gobbler and the next to come in was an adult hen. The poults hadn't even sounded off yet. So you can't always go by the textbooks."

FALL TURKEY PATTERNS

Familiarizing yourself with the day-to-day pattern of turkeys in the fall can be a great help in locating them when you are hunting. It can be especially helpful to find their roosting spots.

"It's good to be in the woods at dusk in the fall.

Familiarizing yourself with the daily patterns of turkeys in the fall can help greatly in locating them when you are hunting.

If you are quiet, you can hear the birds flying up into trees to roost. If you can scatter them off the roost in the evening, just at dusk, (even if they fly only 50 yards to a different tree to roost) they'll definitely want to get back together in the morning. They will often be so hot to get together again that they'll start calling right after fly-down. Sit at the location where you scattered them and you might have the birds come in without even having to call."

Rely on others for help in locating the autumn birds, Hollister suggests. "Rural letter carriers and school bus drivers are good scouts. So are bowhunters, who will be sitting quietly in their treestands until dark and might see or hear birds go on roost. If you know a coon hunter, ask him to inform you if he finds or scatters a flock of roosted birds while hunting at night. That could lead to a great hunting situation in the morning ... if you don't mind being called in the middle of the night." There are some inconveniences worth putting up with when it comes to hunting turkeys in the fall—if you really want to get your bird.

Getting close to the flock is vital for a good scatter. Shooting over the birds' heads will often send them in different directions, which is what you want.

Dogging It for Turkeys

Though a lot of different game birds are hunted with the help of dogs, few people realize that autumn turkeys could be one of them. "Hunting for turkeys with dogs probably began in Virginia in the early 1900s," speculates J. T. Byrne of Bedford County, Virginia.

What does a turkey dog do? If it is performing at its best, the dog will range in a 300- to 600-yard radius from the hunters while it seeks turkeys. It will come back to the hunters every 10 to 15 minutes, then the

Bird dogs aren't just for pheasants, quail or grouse anymore. Combine the right traits—either by luck or by a careful breeding plan—and you've got a turkey dog!

hunters will move along slowly while the dog advances into a fresh circle. If all goes as planned, the hunters will eventually hear barking.

"It's difficult for a person to sneak up on turkeys, break up the flock and really scatter the birds," explains Byrne, "but dogs are natural predators. They can get close, and their bark can send the turkeys in all directions."

J. T. and his father, John, have bred a line of turkey dogs. They combined the traits of various misfits for just the right "fit," so to speak. J. T. relates, "We had a coon- and bear-hunting Plott hound on the farm. If he barked at night, there was likely a coon around. But if he barked during the day, you could bet there was a turkey nearby. Another fellow had an English pointer that hunted turkeys but ranged too far for wingshooting and didn't bark like the Plott. The last link was an English setter that wouldn't hold a point on quail and barked at the flush." Breed a far-ranging hound that barks at turkeys and a setter that doesn't hold point and sounds off at the flush, then add a turkey-hunting pointer to the gene pool, and you've got a turkey dog.

When the circling turkey dogs bark, they are signaling a scatter. If the hunter is standing quietly, he might even hear the wingbeats of the fleeing birds. After the hunter locates the general area where his barking dog flushed the birds, the adventure takes on all the subtleties of a traditional fall turkey hunt—except for what to do with the dog.

"I'll take out a camouflaged duffle bag, put the dog in the bag, zip it up so that only his head is out of the bag, comfortably tuck him between my legs—and he goes to sleep," describes Pete Clare of Turkey Trot Acres in New York, where J. T. Byrne has worked as a guide.

Fall turkey hunting with dogs is not legal in all states, so check individual states' regulations to be sure.

PURSUING THE SLAM

Many turkey hunters consider achieving the Grand Slam—tagging a member of each of the United States's four huntable turkey subspecies—the accomplishment of a lifetime. To qualify for the Grand Slam, a hunter might take a lifetime to succeed, counting birds taken in various years. Harvesting all four subspecies in one year, then, might be the ultimate form of making the Slam.

The lofty goal would seemingly require a huge investment in dollars for airline travel, guide service and hunting-lodge accommodations. Not necessarily so. Enter Jeff Budz, a turkey-hunting fanatic from Boulder, Colorado. Since he began hunting turkeys in the late 1980s, he has recorded seven Grand Slams, including two years in which he doubled up on the feat.

PLANNING YOUR HUNT

"People have to ask themselves, 'How much time and how much money do I have?'" Budz says. "If they have time and the money, then they should get on the phone. They'll be able to make arrangements for all facets of their hunt. If they don't have time to plan economical hunts, then they'll have to spend more money. If they do have time, they could spend less money and go to public hunting areas."

Budz has followed the latter route, concentrating his investment in time rather than money. It has obviously paid off. "I start my research well before the season, making phone calls. I always try to talk to the turkey specialist at a state fish and game department. They are usually a big help, and they may even send me maps where they've penciled in hot spots."

"I also research which states have drawings and what the deadlines are. I much prefer to hunt states where I can simply get my turkey-hunting license or permit over the counter when I arrive there, but if I'm hunting a state or an

The elements of a Slam: Merriam's (top), Eastern (middle left), Florida (middle right) and Rio Grande (bottom) wild turkeys.

area with a lottery, I want to make sure I have my paperwork in on time."

But long-term planning is not the only way Budz has cashed in on public hunting opportunities. "I always have my road atlas with me, and it shows lots of green patches for national forests and other public lands. I had lined up some private property to hunt in Montana last spring, but when I was an hour away from my destination I got word that my hunting opportunity there had fallen through. Sure, I was disappointed, but I simply opened the atlas, found a green area on the Montana map that said 'national forest' and headed there. I stopped in at the ranger's office and asked him where I should go. That was on a Sunday, and that evening I roosted some birds. I got a beautiful tom on Monday morning at 6:15."

Another great map tool is the *DeLorme Atlas & Gazetteer* for the state you're hunting. It shows all the roads a standard atlas would, plus much more detail.

SWEET SUCCESS

Budz attributes his success to hard work—from planning the hunt to actually executing it. "I remember when I headed out to Florida in 1995 to begin my Grand Slam pursuit for that year by getting the Florida subspecies. I had been pointed toward a public hunting area south of Orlando the year before, where I had gotten a jake. Now I arrived four days before the season. I put on my beat-up tennis shoes and worn camouflage clothing, and I walked miles and miles. It paid off when the season opened with two toms in the first three days."

"Success," Budz remarks, "is directly correlated to the miles you put on." If your feet hurt by just thinking about his advice, take consolation in his additional words: "It gets easier through the years."

Budz has found that through experience, he can better identify where birds will be in the public areas he hunts. He has also learned to ask the right questions of his contacts along the way to help avoid wasted miles. He repeats that knowledgeable staff at state fish and game agencies can

About the Expert

Jeff Budz is a contractor based in Boulder, Colorado. He is in his early 30s, single and devoted to turkey hunting. Budz didn't shoot his first turkey until 1989, admitting that he knew little of turkey hunting when he and his friend went afield that day. He's learned fast, however, accomplishing the Grand Slam seven times, including five years in a row, and double Grand Slams in two of those years. Most remarkable of all, perhaps, is that most of this hunting has been done on a shoestring budget on public lands.

help you home in on hot spots.

If it is getting easier for Budz, there's no telling what his future accomplishments might be. One year, Budz harvested six birds, including one of each subspecies. The next year, he completed his first double Grand Slam, then repeated the accomplishment three years later. As of this writing, he has gotten at least one Slam every year for the last 5 years, and he can readily recite the states where he harvested his birds. The list reads like an atlas: Alabama, Arkansas, Colorado, Florida, Georgia, Illinois, Iowa, Missouri, Montana, Nebraska, Oklahoma, South Dakota, Texas and Wyoming!

WHERE TO GO

Because Florida—the sole state that the Florida, or Osceola, subspecies inhabits—only allows a

Recording a Grand Slam

The National Wild Turkey Federation began keeping records of harvested turkeys in 1982. Free turkey registration packets are available upon request. Completing the one-page registration form and sending in $10 allows a hunter to register any wild turkey that he or she has harvested. After the registration has been reviewed and accepted, the date is placed in the NWTF's records. In addition to covering the cost of data entry, the $10 fee entitles the hunter to a certificate and lapel pin for the individual species. Hunters who achieve the Grand Slam receive special lapel pins commemorating the achievement.

The NWTF reports that only 259 Grand Slams were recorded from 1982 through mid-December 1998, though certainly more have been accomplished. But since 1996, the number of slams being certified annually has increased. Either hunters are pursuing Slams with more fervor, or they're just taking the time to register their accomplishments.

You can contact the National Wild Turkey Federation at P.O. Box 530, Edgefield, SC 29824-0530, or call them at (800) THE-NWTF.

---

total of two gobblers to be harvested in a season, accomplishing more than a double Grand Slam in one year is currently impossible.

Which states would Budz recommend to someone seeking the Grand Slam hunt? "Of course, they're going to have to go to Florida. After that it depends on where they are geographically located and how far they can travel. For the Eastern, I recommend Missouri. It is stunning country; there are lots of birds, and permits are sold over the counter. And they've changed their rules a little bit so that now, instead of a two-week season in which you can take one tom in each week, the season is three weeks long, and if you don't take a tom the first week, you can take two in the second or third week. For the Merriam's, I'd say Nebraska; it is incredible! For the Rio, I'd say Texas and Oklahoma, if you can get onto private property. There are tons of birds and it doesn't have to cost as much to hunt as you might think. There are opportunities for under $100. But for public land, there are a lot of public over-the-counter opportunities in Kansas. Oklahoma has some too."

For Budz, the memories have come in volume. With all the accomplishments he has achieved, it is interesting to learn what he considers memorable. "The whole allure of the Grand Slam to me is that I have to go to four distinct areas. So, yes, it is the different people I've met, the places I've gone, the sights and sounds and smells, the food, the dialects, the terrain. It's the knowledge I've gained and the mistakes I've made. And the adrenaline rushes from the different hunts."

"The hunting memories are either of the highs or lows, either when you really messed up or really did something right—'Oh, my gosh, I got him!' or 'Oh, my gosh, he got away!'"

THE BUDZ METHOD

Being self-employed, Jeff Budz plans his vacation time for turkey season. By sleeping in his vehicle, eating food he packed at home and hunting mainly on public lands, he minimizes expenses. By keeping himself in top physical condition, he can both go the extra mile and rise one

more morning—the morning that may bring him a gobbler—before the sun does. By researching his destinations, he is well prepared before he ever arrives.

That's one man's formula for successfully achieving the Grand Slam. It might be something you can adapt to your own lifestyle. At the very least, you can put some of his ideas and strategies to work to help you take a subspecies you've not harvested before.

For More Information on Licensing

The following can provide more information on licensing for wild turkey hunting within their respective borders. Many seasons are limited in area, number of permits, etc., and for many hunts, applications must be submitted well in advance of the season. Some fall seasons are held only when turkey population levels support such a hunt. Be sure to request all available information.

S	=	Spring hunting season offered		*R*	=	Rio Grande subspecies available
F	=	Fall hunting season offered		*M*	=	Merriam's subspecies available
E	=	Eastern subspecies available		*G*	=	Gould's subspecies available
FL	=	Florida subspecies available		*O*	=	Ocellated species available

UNITED STATES

Alabama Dept. of Conservation
  and Natural Resources
64 N. Union St.
Montgomery, AL 36130
(334) 242-3468
E, S&F

Arizona Game and Fish
  Department
2221 W. Greenway Rd.
Phoenix, AZ 85023
(602) 789-4006 & (602) 942-3000
M, S&F

Arkansas Game and
  Fish Commission
License Section
#2 Natural Resources Dr.
Little Rock, AR 72205
(501) 223-6300
E, S&F

California Dept. of Fish & Game:
  License and Revenue Branch
3211 South St.
Sacramento, CA 95816
(916) 227-2244 or
24-hour recording, (916) 227-2266
M&R, S&F

Colorado Div. of Wildlife
6060 Broadway
Denver, CO 80216
(303) 297-1192
M&R, S&F

Connecticut Dept. of
  Environmental Protection
Licensing & Revenue
79 Elm St.
Hartford, CT 06106
(860) 424-3105
E, S&F

(Continued...)

145   Hunting Strategies, Techniques & Tactics

Delaware Div. of Fish & Wildlife
89 Kings Hwy.
Dover, DE 19903
(302) 739-5297
E, S

Florida Game & Fresh Water
    Fish Commission:
    Information
620 S. Meridian St.
Tallahassee, FL 32399
(904) 488-4676
E&F, S&F

Georgia Dept. of Natural Resources:
    Wildlife Resources Division
2070 U.S. Hwy. 278, SE
Social Circle, GA 30279
(770) 918-6401
E, S

Hawaii Dept. of Fish & Wildlife
1151 Punchbowl St.
Honolulu, HI 96813
(808) 587-0166
R, S&F

Idaho Fish and Game Dept.
P.O. Box 25, 600 S. Walnut
Boise, ID 83707
(208) 334-3700
M&R, S&F

Illinois Dept. of Natural Resources:
    Permit Office
P.O. Box 19446
Springfield, IL 62794-9446
(217) 782-7305
E, S&F

Indiana Dept. of Natural Resources
402 W. Washington St.
Indianapolis, IN 46204
(317) 232-4080
E, S

Iowa Dept. of Natural Resources:
    License Bureau
Wallace State Office Bldg.
E. 9th & Grand Ave.
Des Moines, IA 50319-0034
(515) 774-2958
E, S&F

Kansas Wildlife & Parks
512 E. 25th Ave.
Pratt, KS 66801
(316) 672-5911
E&R, S&F

Kentucky Dept. of Fish & Wildlife
#1 Game Farm Rd.
Frankfort, KY 40601
(502) 564-4336
E, S&F

Louisiana Dept. of Wildlife
    & Fisheries
P.O. Box 98000
Baton Rouge, LA 70898-9000
(504) 765-2346
E, S

Maine Dept. of Inland
    Fisheries & Wildlife
Station 41
284 State St.
Augusta, ME 04333
(207) 287-5252
E, S

Maryland Dept. of Natural
    Resources: Licensing Office
Annapolis Service Center
580 Taylor Ave., B-1
Annapolis, MD 21401
(410) 260-8200
E, S&F

Massachusetts Division of Fisheries
    and Wildlife
Rt. 135, North Dr.
Westboro, MA 01581
(508) 792-7270 ext. 124
E, S&F

Michigan Dept. of Natural Resources:
    Wildlife Division
P.O. Box 30044
Lansing, MI 48909
(517) 373-1263
E, S&F (Fall is always dependent on
    population levels)

Minnesota Dept. of Natural
    Resources
License Bureau
500 Lafayette Rd.
St. Paul, MN 55155-4026
(651) 296-4506
E, S&F

Mississippi Dept. of Wildlife,
    Fisheries & Parks
P.O. Box 451
Jackson, MS 39205-0451
(601) 364-2152
E, S&F

Missouri Dept. of Conservation
P.O. Box 180
Jefferson City, MO 65102
(573) 751-4115
E, S&F

Montana Dept. of Fish,
    Wildlife & Parks
P.O. Box 200701
Helena, MT 59620-0701
(406) 444-2535
M, S&F

Nebraska Game and
    Parks Commission
P.O. Box 30370
Lincoln, NE 68503
(402) 471-0641
E&M, S&F

Nevada Dept. of Conservation
    and Natural Resources
Division of Wildlife—License
P.O. Box 10678
Reno, NV 89520
(702) 688-1500
R&M, S&F

New Hampshire Fish & Game Dept.
2 Hazen Dr.
Concord, NH 03301
(603) 271-3421
E, S&F

New Jersey Division of Fish,
    Game & Wildlife
P.O. Box 400
Trenton, NJ 08625-0400
(609) 292-2965
E, S&F

New Mexico Dept. of Game & Fish
P.O. Box 25112
Santa Fe, NM 87504
(505) 827-7885
M&R, S&F

New York Dept.
    of Environmental Conservation:
    Division of Fish, Wildlife &
    Marine Resources
50 Wolf Rd., Room 151
Albany, NY 12233-4790
(518) 457-3521
E, S&F

North Carolina Wildlife
    Resources Commission
512 N. Salisbury St.
Raleigh, NC 27604-1188
(919) 733-7291
E, S&F

North Dakota Game & Fish Dept.
100 N. Bismarck Expressway
Bismarck, ND 58501-5095
(701) 328-6300
E&M, S&F

Ohio Dept. of Natural Resources:
    Division of Wildlife
1840 Belcher Dr.
Columbus, OH 43224
(614) 265-7040
E, S&F

Oklahoma Dept. of
    Wildlife Conservation
P.O. Box 53465
Oklahoma City, OK 73152
(405) 521-4627
E&R, S&F

Oregon Dept. of Fish & Wildlife
License Section
2501 SW 1st Ave.
Portland, OR 97207
(503) 872-5275
M&R, S&F

Pennsylvania Game Commission
2001 Elmerton Ave.
Harrisburg, PA 17110-9797
(717) 787-7015
E, S&F

Rhode Island Division of
    Fish & Wildlife
Stedman Govt. Center
4808 Tower Hill Rd.
Wakefield, R.I. 02879
(401) 789-3094
E, S

South Carolina Department of
    Natural Resources
P.O. Box 167
Columbia, SC 29202
(803) 734-3833
E, S

South Dakota Game,
    Fish & Parks Dept.
412 W. Missouri
Pierre, SD 57501
(605) 773-3485
E, M&R, S&F

Tennessee Wildlife Resources Agency
P.O. Box 40747
Nashville, TN 37204
(615) 781-6500
E, S&F

Texas Parks & Wildlife Dept.
Public Hunting
4200 Smith School Rd.
Austin, TX 78744
(512) 389-4505
E, M&R, S&F

Utah Dept. of Natural Resources:
    Division of Wildlife Resources
1594 W. N. Temple, Ste. 2110
Box 146301
Salt Lake City, UT 84114-6301
(801) 538-4700
M&R, S

Vermont Dept. of Fish & Wildlife
103 S. Main St., 10 S.
Waterbury, VT 05671
(802) 241-3700
E, S&F

Virginia Dept. of Game &
    Inland Fisheries
Box 11104
Richmond, VA 23230
(804) 367-1000
E, S&F

Washington Dept. of Fish & Wildlife
600 Capitol Way N.
Olympia, WA 98501
(360) 902-2200
E, M&R, S&F

West Virginia Division of
    Natural Resources
Wildlife Resources Section
Capitol Complex
Bldg. 3, Room 812
Charleston, WV 25305
(304) 558-3380
E, S&F

Wisconsin Dept. of
    Natural Resources
License Section
P.O. Box 7921
Madison, WI 53707
(608) 266-2105
E, S&F

Wyoming Game & Fish
License Section
5400 Bishop Blvd.
Cheyenne, WY 82006-0001
(307) 777-4600
M, S&F

CANADA

Alberta Environmental
    Protection Fisheries and
    Wildlife Management Division
Main Floor
9915 118th St.
Edmonton, Alberta
Canada T5K 2G6
(403) 427-6975
M, S (residents only)

British Columbia Ministry of
    Environment, Land and Parks
Wildlife Branch
P.O. Box 9374
Stn Prov Gov
Victoria, British Columbia
Canada V8W 9M4
(250) 387-9739
*M, S (residents only for limited
lottery; nonresidents may hunt
with guides who have been
assigned an annual quota)*

Manitoba Dept. of Natural Resources
    Wildlife Branch
200 Saulteaux Crescent, Box 24
Winnipeg, Manitoba
Canada R3J 3W3
(204) 945-6808
E-M Hybrid, S&F (residents only)

Ontario Ministry of
    Natural Resources
P.O. Box 7000
Peterborough, Ontario
Canada K9J 8M5
(705) 755-1932
E, S

MEXICO

*George Wright, Outfitter
149 Needmore Rd.
Princeton, KY 42445
(502) 365-7278
G, O

*Indio Outfitters
P.O. Box 1559
Chihuahua, Mexico
011-52-14-191919
G

*These are sources of information, but
their listing does not necessarily imply
an endorsement of their services.*

Chapter 5

AFTER THE SHOT

When you bag a wild turkey, you probably reach the pinnacle of your bird-hunting experience. Of course, you make other precious gains along the way—beautiful country, closeup views of wildlife, special moments with companions ... the list goes on. Just as you enjoyed these special benefits before you tagged your turkey, you can expect other delights after the shooting, congratulations and picture-taking are all over.

Almost anyone who tastes a well-prepared meal featuring wild turkey has to come back for seconds. Most people who have viewed a professionally-mounted turkey have to stop and admire the bird's beauty and the skill of the person who preserved it. The meal provides a fleeting reward to be savored and remembered. The wide possibilities for utilizing the bird—from life-size and tail-fan mounts to jewelry and wingbone calls—are to be treasured for decades.

So it's true—the wild turkey can reward its victor long after the moment of the kill, but soon after that moment the hunter must properly handle the bird and treat it with the respect it warrants.

How to get the most from the wild turkey in the kitchen falls under the expertise of Sylvia G. Bashline, whose appreciative fans have read her cooking columns in major sporting magazines and best-selling books. Tips on a variety of ways to make a lasting memento of your wild turkey come from Charles Haviland, an award-winning taxidermist.

You'll learn how to care for your bird in the stages leading up to preservation or kitchen preparation. You'll also discover how to mount a tail fan yourself and how to cook a turkey that will have your diners looking forward, almost as much as you will, to the next turkey hunting season.

PRESERVING THE EXPERIENCE

*T*urkey hunting is a memorable experience, whether or not you tag a gobbler. If you do, however, you might want to commemorate the hunt by preserving your bird. It may be your first wild turkey, and that warrants special treatment. Perhaps it is your largest, or maybe just the most difficult. Countless factors can make a turkey a trophy you wish to preserve, and you have many options for how you might save the memory.

But no matter which option you choose, you must be able to give the taxidermist a specimen worth preserving. Even if you are simply preserving the beard and the tail fan—something you can do at home—you still must know what to do to assure a prime specimen.

MAKE YOUR SHOT COUNT

"Though it might not be advice you would expect from a taxidermist," remarks Charles Haviland, "my first words of wisdom are to make sure you pattern your gun before you go hunting. That way you know how far you can shoot to get the killing shot you desire. What you are after is a clean, one-shot kill."

"As a taxidermist, I get to see just how thick the turkey's body feathers and fat are. That's a lot to shoot through, especially if you are at a long range."

From the taxidermist's perspective, Haviland doesn't think it matters what size shot you use; it's where you put it that counts.

"The best shot is the head. Not only is that a lethal zone, but if anything happens to the head, we always have spare freeze-dried heads. That is the easiest part of the turkey to fix or replace. On the other hand, if you start blowing patches of feathers out of the bird, then patching and replacing gets a little tricky."

"You might want to avoid shooting when the tom has his tail feathers fanned. He has his head tucked in then, so you have a greater risk of damaging the feathers in the chest and back. If you can, shoot while the bird is gobbling or while he has his head up to look around." When the bird gobbles, it typically folds up its tail feathers and sticks its head out.

Often a turkey will not simply drop at the point of impact and die immediately. Even if it doesn't run, it often will violently flap and thrash against the ground. What should a hunter do then to dispatch his bird, yet not damage it?

"Don't shoot it again!" Haviland pleads. "At close range, you may damage it beyond repair. I would recommend simply letting nature take its course. The bird will usually die in minutes, even seconds."

Further advice here, if you choose to follow Haviland's guideline: Stay close to the bird, gun at ready. What you don't want is for the bird to get up and run or fly away. If it seems like it's going to get up and do just that, deliver a finishing shot; a slightly damaged bird is better than a lost bird.

"I've seen hunters do irreparable damage by jumping on their bird, wringing its neck and grabbing the tail. Next thing you know they have a handful of feathers because they pulled the tail

A head shot will kill a wild turkey quickly and neatly.

feathers and broke wing feathers trying to hold the bird down."

"But if it looks like the bird isn't going to stop flapping, you might want to do something. You have to be careful of reaching for the bird because of its sharp spurs. I've had people come into my studio with their arms raked. One-inch spurs can do damage."

There is no great way to dispatch a dying turkey, Haviland says. "Wring its neck only if you have to," he advises. "Just try to be as gentle as possible."

About the Expert

Charles Haviland was 14 years old when he began his taxidermy career. He ultimately became licensed in his homestate of New York and joined taxidermy associations in both Connecticut and New York.

Both he and his wife Maura, with whom he shares Grouse Hill Taxidermy in Putnam Valley, New York, conduct seminars (including one on turkeys) for other professional taxidermists.

The Havilands have won major awards, including Best of Show and Taxidermists' Choice, from their two state organizations. Not only do the Havilands' preserve turkeys, Charles also hunts them.

After the Shot

Once it's down, treat your trophy right by utilizing the advice in this book.

FIELD DRESSING AND IMMEDIATE CARE

The next step depends on what you might want to do with your bird and how soon you'll be able to get it to the taxidermist. If you aren't thinking about a life-size mount, which requires the full skin of your bird, then you should field dress your turkey. This would also be the case, even if you do desire a full mount, if you will not be able to get to the taxidermist until the next day or later.

"Make a small cut just below the breast plate all the way to the anal vent," Haviland advises. "Then remove the innards." (See the diagram below for more field-dressing details.) Turkeys are heavily feathered birds, and that incision is easily repaired, the taxidermist assures.

You can now carefully tuck your prize into your vest or carry him by the legs, but do not carry him by the neck. Even carrying the bird by the legs requires some degree of care because a standing mount on broken legs won't look very good, Haviland warns. Although he urges you to keep the bird as clean as possible, don't be too concerned about minimal amounts of blood getting on the feathers if it is earmarked for the taxidermist's studio; just wash it off before the blood dries. "The taxidermist turns the bird's skin inside out, then defats and washes it," Haviland explains, "so most of the blood comes off."

When you get back to camp or your vehicle, you should think about the next step. "Put the bird on ice or keep it cool the best way you can, whether that's in a refrigerator or cool shade. If you can't get the turkey to the taxidermist the same day, then freeze it."

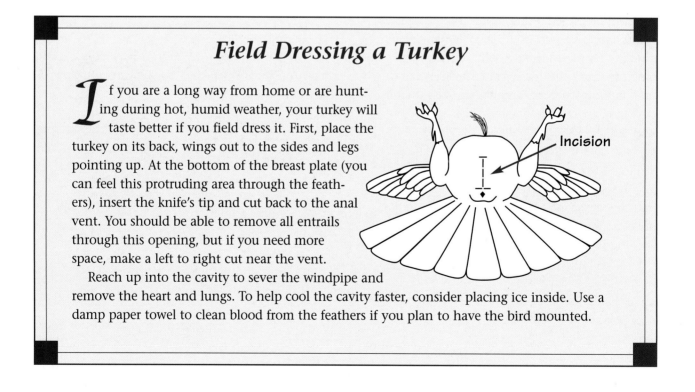

Field Dressing a Turkey

*I*f you are a long way from home or are hunting during hot, humid weather, your turkey will taste better if you field dress it. First, place the turkey on its back, wings out to the sides and legs pointing up. At the bottom of the breast plate (you can feel this protruding area through the feathers), insert the knife's tip and cut back to the anal vent. You should be able to remove all entrails through this opening, but if you need more space, make a left to right cut near the vent.

Reach up into the cavity to sever the windpipe and remove the heart and lungs. To help cool the cavity faster, consider placing ice inside. Use a damp paper towel to clean blood from the feathers if you plan to have the bird mounted.

Incision

Haviland says that if a customer brings the turkey to him fresh, he'll skin it right there and return the whole turkey or cut off the breast so the customer can enjoy the meat.

SKINNING FOR A MOUNT

Sometimes a hunter can't get his bird to the taxidermist right away. He should skin the bird himself, which allows him a variety of options from full mount down to a simple tail fan when he finally decides what he would like the taxidermist to do.

"Skinning is not that difficult," Haviland begins. "Cut through the skin from the chest down to the anal vent, following the ridge of the breast. Then start peeling the skin back. When you get to the neck, skin it, then cut the neck bone and flesh, but don't cut through the skin."

"Next, you'll hit the wings. Dislocate the wing bone from the body. Then work your way down to the legs and dislocate them from the body, leaving the bones in the wings and legs intact. Then, when you get to the tail, cut the tail off from the body, leaving it attached to the skin. Then you have the whole skin, with the leg bones and wings intact. When you are finished with the skinning process, you'll simply tuck the attached head and neck into the skin, which you will roll up. Just fold it up carefully, bag it, and as soon as you can, freeze it. It won't take up much room in this form, you'll have the meat to eat, and you can get the skin to the taxidermist at your convenience."

Personally delivering your bird to a local taxidermist is easy. Shipping it to a favored studio a distance away is more of a logistical challenge.

"Be sure to roll up the skin and freeze it solid, packing newspaper around it when boxing the prize. Call and let the taxidermist know you are sending the bird, which should be shipped for either overnight or second-day delivery. Either is fine, because it takes a day or two to thaw the bird under fall or early-spring conditions."

Following are detailed instructions, and diagrams, on how you can skin a turkey for a full-size mount.

Skinning for a Mount

Place the turkey on its back with legs and wings out to each side. Insert your knife at the end of the breastplate and cut to the anal vent opening. Start on each side of this opening to peel the skin from the body. (When you are all finished, legs, wings, head, tail and the body skin will all be attached.)

First, cut through the skin from the chest to the anal vent. Start peeling the skin back. When you get to the neck, skin it and cut the neck bone and flesh, but don't cut through the skin. The head remains attached to the neck skin, and the neck skin to the body skin.

Next, skin down the back of the bird toward the wings and legs. Dislocate the wing bone from the body, then work down to the legs and dislocate them from the body, leaving the bones and wings intact.

Then, disconnect the tail from the body, leaving the tail attached to the skin. If you have not completely skinned the back of the bird at this point, do so now so that you can remove the entire skin.

Try gently to remove blood from the feathers with a damp cloth or towel. A taxidermist can usually remove blood from feathers when processing the skin.

(1) **Initial Cuts**
Make initial cuts. Begin peeling skin toward head (blue lines).

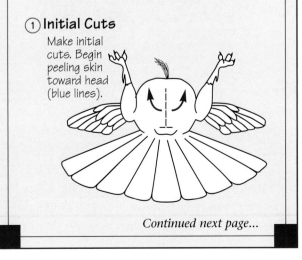

Continued next page...

Continued from previous page

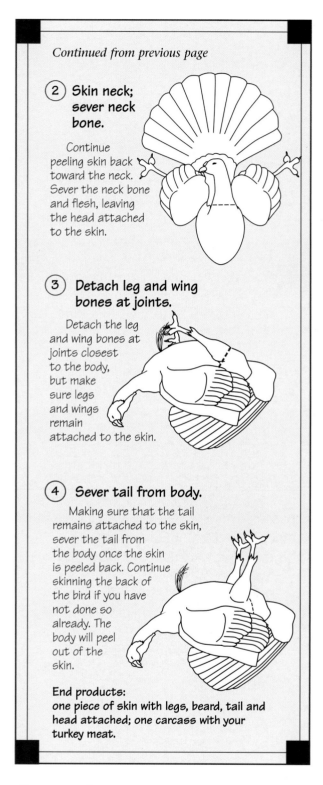

② Skin neck; sever neck bone.

Continue peeling skin back toward the neck. Sever the neck bone and flesh, leaving the head attached to the skin.

③ Detach leg and wing bones at joints.

Detach the leg and wing bones at joints closest to the body, but make sure legs and wings remain attached to the skin.

④ Sever tail from body.

Making sure that the tail remains attached to the skin, sever the tail from the body once the skin is peeled back. Continue skinning the back of the bird if you have not done so already. The body will peel out of the skin.

End products: one piece of skin with legs, beard, tail and head attached; one carcass with your turkey meat.

If the hunter can't get his trophy to the taxidermist soon after the kill, he should skin the bird himself.

TROPHY OPTIONS

Once you do get the skin to the taxidermist, the decision will be made as to what you want done. "You can have a life-size mount," Haviland describes, "which can be in any position you can dream of. One of the most popular poses is the tom gobbling on the roost because it hangs on the wall, and it is in a 'closed-up' position. In other words, for a full mount, it doesn't take over a room. Then, of course, there's strutting and standing and all of the other positions."

"You can get a half–mount, which is the chest of the bird, with the head and the fan. Even there, you have a choice of the wings out or hammered down as if in strut."

In all these cases, the skin is slipped over a foam-plastic body and, sometimes, a head. In some cases, legs and heads can be artificial yet realistic casts.

"One new option is an artificial head and chest in front of your actual tail fan put on an attractive plaque. Tail fan and beard mounts on an oak or walnut panel, with a laser-engraved turkey on the panel, look really sharp. Of course, many hunters simply elect to hang their tail mount on the wall, adorned by the beard. One way to commemorate a Grand Slam would be simply to hang the beards on a single, decorated panel. You might want to cut off and glue the spurs to the panel and perhaps decorate it with one of the tail fans as the background. Some of those commercially made decorative panels hold up to 10 beards."

The options are limited only by the hunter's and taxidermist's imaginations.

"Even the legs are an option. Some hunters make jewelry out of the spurs. You simply cut the spur from the leg with a hacksaw and peel the scaly part off so all you see is hollow bone. Some people boil the spurs in coffee or another coloring agent. I've seen necklaces of spurs."

I recall a friend who cut off the leg of his first gobbler, injected it with formaldehyde and proudly kept the standing leg on his office desk.

Beards by themselves can make a handsome trophy. "Simply cut the beard from the bird. [See diagram below.] It will easily detach. Put a little bit of Borax on the skin attachment to dry this portion. Get a really attractive wrapping thread like you'd use on a fishing rod and wrap the portion of the beard where it attaches to the bird's chest. Varnish the thread as you would on a fishing rod, then put a hook on it so you can hang it on display."

Haviland recognizes that a lot of people simply want to preserve their tail fans, and they can do that themselves. He is happy to share his method for getting the best results. (See "Mount a Tail Fan Yourself" on pages 156-157.)

A life-size mount is one way to preserve your trophy.

He does have a warning for do-it-yourselfers: "The old method was to remove as much of the 'meat' from the base of the tail fan as possible, spread the fan and pin it on a board to dry. To help dry and preserve it, people would rub Borax or salt into the meaty base."

"That method is a crap shoot, because bugs can be a problem. Some people run into the problem;

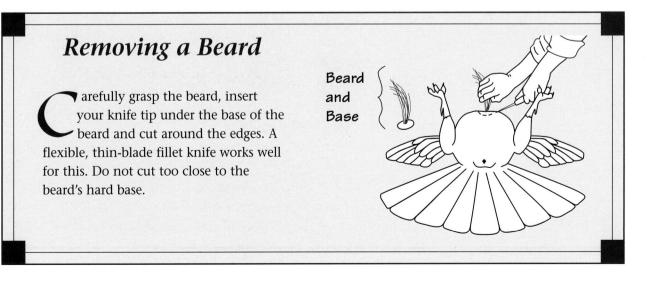

Removing a Beard

Carefully grasp the beard, insert your knife tip under the base of the beard and cut around the edges. A flexible, thin-blade fillet knife works well for this. Do not cut too close to the beard's hard base.

Beard and Base

155

others don't. You never know when a moth is going to leave its larvae on your mount. In my professional opinion, it is a bug feast waiting to happen. And when it does," Haviland says, "with just a touch, feathers will simply fall out."

Care for your mount might be simply an occasional gentle feather dusting. In addition, by dipping that feather duster lightly in paint thinner, Haviland says you will restore a brilliant sheen to the turkey. "If the feathers become a bit frayed," he advises, "try steaming them to restore their original shape."

Commemorating a hunt through preserving your bird presents numerous—almost unlimited—options.

Mount a Tail Fan Yourself

One of the most attractive mementos of a successful turkey hunt is a mount of your turkey's tail feathers, fanned out as they would have been when the gobbler was displaying. Charles Haviland is happy to share his quick, easy, thorough and attractive method for mounting a tail fan yourself.

---

1 *Cut the tail fan from the rest of the bird. Clean away the flesh and fat from the skin and quills of the feathers at the base of the fan. First, peel the skin away from the bone to allow easier access to the flesh you wish to remove.*

2 *With pliers, break the bone in both the front and back of the base of the fan.*

3 *Using a knife, remove as much flesh as possible. Push your knife upward between each quill and scrape all the flesh and fat from between the quills and off the skin flap. Do this on both sides. You might want to use a wire brush to get down to the bare quills.*

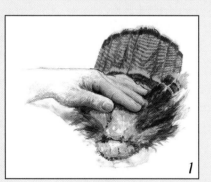

4 On a piece of cardboard, mix the two components of an auto-body filler, such as Bondo—one to two tablespoons of filler and one or two drops of hardener (available inexpensively at auto parts and department stores). Place the base of the fan on the top half of a sheet of waxed paper, then apply the mixed auto-body filler to the base of the fan. Work the compound into the quills, both top and bottom.

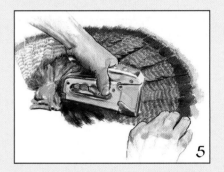

5 Spread out the fan on a board and, with a staple gun, staple over the vein of two or three tail feathers at each end of the fan.

6 Cover the base with the other half of the waxed paper, then place something heavy over the auto-body filler area. In 10 to 15 minutes the compound should be hard. You can use the leftover compound on your piece of cardboard as an indicator of when the mixture on your tail fan has hardened.

7 After the auto bonding compound has hardened, remove the staples and wax paper. If you want to clean off excess filler, it is still soft enough to be shaped and even lightly sanded or filed.

8 After 24 hours, the base will be rock hard and can be drilled. You can put the tail fan on a variety of plaques advertised in magazines or sold by taxidermists. Cover the base and lower portion of the fan with leather or wood, and hang the beard from the base. The options are numerous; the trophy is permanent.

After the Shot

PREPARATION FOR THE KITCHEN

*T*ail fans on the wall are striking. A realistic mount of a gobbler on roost can be breath-taking. A plaque with spurs and beard will evoke pride. But none of these mementos of a successful hunt taste very good, and you sure can't eat feathers. In fact, after you remove the innards when field dressing your bird, the feathers are the next thing to go. To assure the bird you worked so hard to harvest tastes great, here are some tips from one of our country's top game cooks.

MAKE YOUR TURKEY TASTE GREAT

"If you are going to roast your turkey, you need to get the feathers off without destroying the skin," advises Sylvia Bashline, renowned game- and fish-cooking authority. "My favorite way of getting the feathers off is to boil a big pot of water, take it outside and 'slosh' the bird up and down in it for a few minutes to loosen the feathers. Then," she says, "pluck away. It's the best way to loosen the feathers, but take care not to cook the skin in the process," she cautions.

After you have field dressed and plucked your bird, refrigerate it as soon as possible. "Storage in the refrigerator for a day is an option, and for a couple of days it's okay, but after that you really should freeze it."

Most people like to roast their turkey, suggests Bashline, so it is important to keep the skin intact. Others may choose simply to breast out their birds, winding up with skinless breast meat.

"If I had my druthers, you would separate the breast and cook it separately from the legs and the rest of the carcass because those parts really require different cooking times," she remarks.

The legs are always the last part of the turkey to be tenderized by cooking, sometimes at the expense of dried-out breasts. And it's a shame to make that beautiful meat tough and chewy. "That's why you have to keep extra moisture on the breast by basting it often," she explains. "You'll also want to baste it at the end of the cooking period and even use a gravy in the basting. That way, the breast meat will have a moist gravy on it when you are carving."

Bashline says that if you have more than one wild turkey to cook in the same season, you should roast one, and with the other, use one of her favorite recipes for skinless breasts (see *Fried Turkey Breast*).

"I think hunters would be absolutely delighted to discover how moist and delicious the breast meat is when it is sliced and cooked quickly, almost like a steak," she points out. The quick cooking seals in the meat's natural juices.

There are differences between the wild and domestic turkey that become obvious in the kitchen. "One thing people don't realize is the rather meager amount of breast meat on a wild bird compared to the tame turkey that has been bred for a big breast. No, you are not going to get as much breast meat out of a wild turkey—but it's going to be richer and far more flavorful!"

Since a wild turkey is just that—wild, and not fattened up in a barnyard—the wild variety can become dry if not cooked with care.

"One thing that really helps keep it moist is to make your stuffing inside the bird as moist as possible. It is also why keeping the skin intact is essential. You really need that skin to hold the natural moisture in the bird as it cooks. I also like to keep a cheesecloth on top of the skin to help further retain the natural juices."

Many hunters are quick to chop off the wings and legs of their wild turkey, as they have a reputation for being tough. These birds do work for a living, and it's through flying and walking that they commute, so the toughness of these parts discourages cooking attempts.

But Bashline offers recipes that include both and says she loves the legs. "If you waste the legs, you waste all that wonderful flavor that you won't get from any other bird. The upper thigh has a lot of meat. The lower legs do have bones and tendons, but you'll still find tasty meat if you cook them in water with a bouillon cube and a few onions and celery. Just cook them until they are tender. Then strip off the meat and use it in whatever you'd like ... on rice with gravy or pasta or just a hot sandwich. (See recipes on the following pages.) But don't waste it," she emphasizes. "A wild turkey's flavor is too special."

What a great way to get two meals out of one bird—a first meal from the breast, a second from the legs and wings.

About the Expert

Sylvia G. Bashline is the former food columnist for both *Field & Stream* and *Outdoor Life* magazines. In addition, she is the author of three game and fish cookbooks: *Bounty of the Earth Cookbook*, *Savory Game Cookbook* and *Cleaning and Cooking Fish*.

Bashline and her late husband, Jim, traveled the continent hunting and fishing, and she has honed her cooking mastery from the many opportunities she had to prepare the game and fish they harvested.

After the Shot

ROAST TURKEY WITH ORANGE DRESSING

1 wild turkey, plucked
Soft butter
½ cup orange juice
½ cup butter
1 teaspoon orange peel
Orange Dressing (below)

Prepare Orange Dressing. Dry turkey with paper towels. Stuff with Orange Dressing and close the body and neck cavities with skewers. With string, tie the wings close to the body and the legs together. Rub the turkey all over with soft butter. Place a double thickness of cheesecloth over the whole bird, put it on a rack in a roasting pan and place in a preheated 350°F oven. After 30 minutes, reduce heat to 325°F.

Place the orange juice, 1/2 cup butter and orange peel in a small saucepan and heat. Baste every 25 minutes with this mixture. Roast the bird for 20 to 25 minutes per pound until done.

Remove the turkey from the oven and allow it to rest on a heated platter while you make the gravy. Remove the fat from pan juices by skimming with a tablespoon. Pour the remaining juices into a saucepan and thicken with flour or cornstarch mixed with water. Darken the gravy a little by adding a small amount of a browning and seasoning sauce. Add salt and pepper if desired.

Orange Dressing

¼ cup chopped onion
½ cup chopped celery
1 cup sliced mushrooms
¼ cup butter or margarine
1 orange, peeled, seeded and diced
1 teaspoon grated orange peel
½ teaspoon poultry seasoning
1 chicken bouillon cube
6 cups dry bread cubes
Orange juice

In a large skillet, heat the butter and fry the onion, celery and mushrooms for about 7 minutes or until tender. Add the diced orange, orange peel, poultry seasoning and bouillon cube. Crush the cube and mix well. Add the bread and toss. Add enough orange juice to make a very moist stuffing (the moisture helps keep the meat juicy). Heat well and stuff in the neck and body cavities of the turkey just before roasting. Makes enough dressing for a 10-pound bird.

ROAST TURKEY WITH PEANUTS

10- to 14-pound wild turkey
1 cup butter
½ cup dry white wine
½ cup chicken bouillon
Salt and pepper
Peanut Dressing (below)

Prepare Peanut Dressing. Rub the bird with butter, sprinkle with salt and pepper and stuff it with Peanut Dressing. Use skewers to close the body opening. Place the bird in a roasting pan and cover completely with cheesecloth. Mix the rest of the butter, the wine and bouillon together and use it to baste the turkey every 25 minutes until you can baste with pan juices. Place in a 350°F oven for the first hour, reduce heat to 325°F for the remaining time. Roast the bird for 20 to 25 minutes per pound.

Peanut Dressing

2 stalks celery, chopped
1 onion, finely chopped
3 teaspoons butter, melted

3 cups roasted peanuts
4½ cups dry bread crumbs
2 eggs, beaten
1 cup chicken bouillon
½ cup white wine
½ teaspoon sage
  Pepper to taste

Sauté the celery and onion in the butter. Chop the peanuts coarsely and mix all ingredients together. The dressing should be quite moist to help the turkey keep its moisture. This is enough dressing for a 12-pound wild turkey.

FRIED TURKEY BREAST

1 turkey breast
½ cup cooking oil
½ cup dry vermouth
1 teaspoon celery salt
1 teaspoon chervil (or parsley flakes)
½ teaspoon savory
  Salt and pepper
  Parsley sprigs

With a sharp fillet knife, separate the meat from the breast bone, scraping the bone to get all the meat. Cut the meat, against the grain, into ¼-inch-thick slices. If possible, remove the white tendon that runs down the middle of the breast before slicing. If it doesn't pull out easily, you can remove it as you slice. Put the slices in a nonmetal bowl with the cooking oil, vermouth, celery salt and chervil or parsley flakes. Mix well and marinate for about 3 hours. Heat a large frying pan and add 3 tablespoons of the marinade. Over high heat, fry the turkey slices quickly for about 2 minutes on each side, turning with a spatula. Don't overcook or the meat will be tough. Add more marinade if necessary. Place the cooked meat on a heated platter,

in a preheated 150°F oven, to keep it warm until all pieces are done. Serve immediately, garnishing with parsley sprigs. Two pounds of breast meat will serve 4.

HOT TURKEY SANDWICH

1 wild turkey with legs and wings
¼ cup finely chopped onion
¼ cup finely chopped celery with leaves
1 beef bouillon cube
1 bay leaf
  Flour
  Browning and seasoning sauce

Remove the turkey skin and cut off the legs and wings. Cut the carcass into manageable pieces with game scissors. Put them all in a large pot with the onion, celery, bouillon cube and bay leaf, and cover all with water. Cover and bring to a boil; reduce heat and simmer until the leg meat is fork-tender. Remove the meat and allow it to cool. Then pull it off the bones in large chunks. Remove the bay leaf from the broth. Thicken the broth by putting flour in a large jar with some cool broth and shaking well. (The amount of flour depends on how much broth there is. Try ⅓ cup at first.) Pour the flour mixture into the broth, heating and stirring until it thickens. Add a little browning and seasoning sauce to darken the gravy. (The dish can be held at this point for an hour or so.) Heat the gravy until it's bubbling hot and add meat. Count on at least one cup of meat per sandwich (more if you like a fat sandwich). While the meat is heating, place a slice of bread on each serving plate. With a slotted spoon, place meat on the bread. Top with another slice of bread and ladle gravy generously over the bread. Serve immediately.

Chapter 6

THE FUTURE OF TURKEY HUNTING

*T*he wild turkey's history on this continent reads like a roller-coaster graph. You've learned about the wild turkey's widespread distribution when Europeans first came to the continent, and you know of the subspecies' plummeting populations into the early twentieth century. Turkey numbers began to rise under the guidance of modern wildlife management, which took advantage of a return of habitat, technological advancements in capturing and transporting live wild turkeys, and concerted financial, spiritual and manual support. Today the wild turkey is hunted in 49 of the 50 states, provinces of Canada and portions of Mexico.

What then does the future hold for this bird now on a spectacular rebound? Rob Keck, executive vice president and chief executive officer of the National Wild Turkey Federation, shares his educated opinion of where wild turkeys and wild turkey hunting are heading in the twenty-first century.

The graph should continue to climb when reflecting turkey and turkey hunter numbers. But that doesn't mean problems don't loom on the horizon; Keck reveals those problems and some potential solutions, inviting you to be part of that solution.

Of course, as turkey hunting interest grows, so will the industry that the sport supports. You've learned about the variety of gear that could help a turkey hunter incorporate success, comfort and safety into every outing. New manufacturers will come on the scene, and products will continue to evolve. To get your database of manufacturers and mail-order outlets started, we have provided an extensive sampling of companies with which you may want to familiarize yourself. You would be wise to build up a library of literature and place yourself on their mailing lists.

It will help you keep pace with the developments in the bright future for which turkey hunting is destined. To keep that future on course, we all have to invest—with money when we can, of course, but more importantly with our time and energy—in the wild turkey and places it calls home.

Looking Ahead

As head of the National Wild Turkey Federation (NWTF), Rob Keck probably has been more involved than anyone else in restoring and expanding turkey range and populations across the continent. His intimate involvement in the past and present management strategies of the wild turkey gives him a unique perspective to draw upon when speculating on the future of the wild turkey, its management and hunting opportunities.

"The wild turkey has proven just about every prognosticator in the turkey world wrong in the last 40 years," he admits. "What was thought to have been ideal habitat 40 years ago turned out to be quite different today. The adaptability of the bird has gone beyond anybody's wildest dreams."

"Back then, it was believed a flock of wild turkeys needed 10,000 acres of contiguous mixed pine and hardwood timber to maximize their numbers. Since then, we've found out how important openings are for reproduction and feeding."

Certainly biologists in Iowa will confess to their mistake. "In the mid-'70s," explains Keck, "biologists there believed their state might be able to hold 1,500 birds because less than four percent of land was in timber. The population of those birds has increased to well over 150,000. In those areas where there is timber along with agriculture, some densities have exceeded 100 birds per square mile."

Birds have expanded into other areas previously thought unlikely habitat for wild turkeys. Adaptability has been the key word in the wild turkey's success. "They are thriving in agricultural areas in Wisconsin and Minnesota. They are expanding into snowbelt states, including areas where annual snowfall may reach 150 inches! Some of the Canadian provinces where turkeys may not have existed before now are supporting wild turkey populations."

"Until as recently as 1997, biologists in Utah thought the state's 20,000 Rio Grandes had filled 95 percent of the believed habitat. Today, those same biologists are amazed at the natural expansion of the Rios. They now think that only five percent of the habitat is filled and look forward to an eventual statewide population of more than 200,000."

Keck says that turkeys have taught wildlife managers one thing: "It's the turkey that tells us where and how far it will expand its range. These expansions are something that will continue to challenge our thinking and our management techniques."

Today, Keck believes there are approximately 4.5 million wild turkeys in the United States, which,

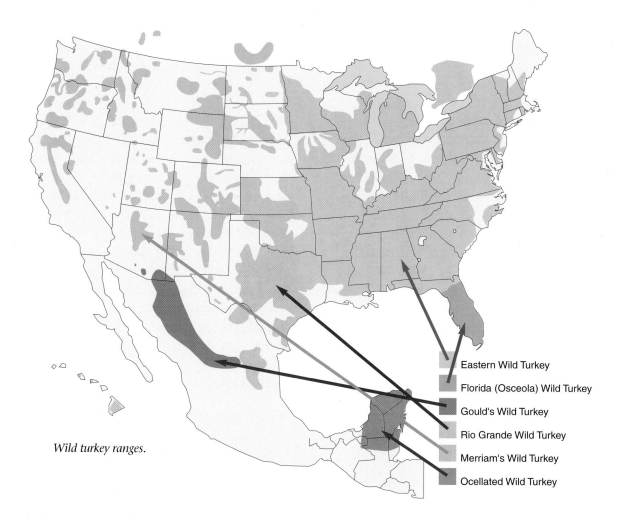

Wild turkey ranges.

Eastern Wild Turkey

Florida (Osceola) Wild Turkey

Gould's Wild Turkey

Rio Grande Wild Turkey

Merriam's Wild Turkey

Ocellated Wild Turkey

he acknowledges, is really only an accumulation of best estimates from each state.

In the U.S., the bird is hunted in 49 states. Alaska is the only state that does not offer wild turkey hunting. "In the U.S., the wild turkey occupies more square miles of range than any other game bird or game animal. In Mexico, the Gould's, Rio Grande and ocellated turkeys are hunted. In Canada, turkeys are found in every province bordering the Lower 48 except New Brunswick, and that province has expressed interest in receiving turkeys the next time turkeys are moved."

According to Keck, limited hunts are held in some of those border provinces. "In Ontario, although there is a drawing, I'm told that virtually every hunter who applies gets a permit. More than 5,000 hunters pursue turkeys in that province alone each year, and 28,000 have passed the mandatory turkey hunting education course held there. There are more than 20,000 birds in

the province, and their restoration program is expanding beyond what the bird's ancestral range might have been."

Expansion of the wild turkey will continue not only in the United States and Canada but perhaps in Mexico—and Europe.

"In fact, in the late '70s birds were transplanted from Vermont to what was then West Germany, along the Rhine River. Those birds increased in numbers, but then they, along with most of the wildlife in the area, had trouble reproducing. They believe it was due to unregulated chemical applications of herbicides and insecticides."

"In Mexico, we are funding research right now by Lovett Williams to better understand the ocellated turkey. We would like to help establish a sport hunting industry to show the people that a wild turkey is worth much more than the $10 market hunters get."

Just as wild turkey numbers have increased

remarkably, so has the number of wild turkey hunters. "Our best numbers show about 2.5 million," reports Keck.

"You hear so many references to the large number of duck hunters in this country," he continues, "but duck stamp sales have not been reaching that 2.5 million level, and not all of them are bought by hunters. So the number of turkey hunters exceeds the count of duck hunters. The opportunities are very widespread. We see the participation numbers continuing to grow across the board, but especially in those emerging states where restoration has been completed in just the last 10 years or so."

"Growth in the western states has been, and will continue to be, great. For one reason, there is a strong parallel between elk hunting and turkey hunting. It's a natural for elk hunters to cross over and hunt spring turkeys because the tactics are so

similar. The two species can even live in the same places, and they respond to the same management techniques." Enough reason to consider the wild turkey a true big game bird.

Keck has taken wild turkeys in all 49 states that offer hunting. Does he think he will ever get to hunt in Alaska? "I think that very well may occur, but unless there is a push by the Alaska Game and Fish Department, we at the NWTF will not pursue that. We have always wanted the state agency to take the lead on wild turkey introductions beyond the ancestral range. Although historical records do not indicate that the wild turkey was indigenous to Alaska, there is some habitat in which they could probably do quite well. We do have a chapter in that state, and there is a lot of interest in turkey hunting. In fact, a Missouri biologist told us that one year 52 successful spring turkey hunters in his state came from Alaska."

Growth—both in the number of turkeys and turkey hunters—is expected to be great in the western states.

Future of Turkey Hunting

North, south, east or west, one word is key to the wild turkey's future—habitat.

Keck thinks the Alaska Game and Fish Department will initiate interest at some point. Some of the Canadian provinces, Keck believes, could get more involved with wild turkey management and improve their hunting even more.

"Pennsylvania was one of the last states to raise and release pen-reared birds, and it stopped that practice in 1981. Many clubs and individuals in Canada are still doing it. It's a waste of time and money. Our federation is willing to bring in and share experts on wild turkey management. Most agencies, however, are underfunded and have a bit of a fear of introductions that seem foreign."

"Agencies must plan and manage. Because when turkeys come on the scene through stocking efforts or by natural expansion, people's interests are going to peak, and they are going to want to hunt. The agencies need to be prepared."

Keck is confident that participation in the great sport of turkey hunting will continue to grow. "As turkey numbers grow, turkey hunter numbers will grow. Birds are expanding into and flourishing in places where there weren't any a few years ago. Birds from West Virginia and Ohio expanded into

Green and Washington counties in Pennsylvania, for example, which the Pennsylvania Game Commission for many years considered marginal for turkeys. That's changed, and they are now the leading counties as far as numbers of harvested birds go."

Another facet of turkey hunting will lead to more growth. "Spring turkey hunting occurs at such a beautiful time of the year." Keck believes mild weather surely contributes to the sport's continued popularity.

Of course, there are a variety of other factors that Keck predicts will contribute to the sport's growth. "For one thing, you don't have to kill a bird to have a successful day. It's the gobble, not the gobbler, that's so prominent. Another reason for future growth is that more women are getting involved, because of their husbands and boyfriends, and many are striking out on their own."

Keck looked at his crystal ball to foresee where turkey management is headed.

One thing he sees is habitat improvement, and he is pleased to see the NWTF play a part with various programs. "Our 'Operation SOS'—Set Out

Seedlings—has volunteers working hand in hand with state wildlife agencies planting a variety of shrubs, trees and other vegetation to help carry turkeys through the difficult winter months in the snowbelt states."

"In the upper Great Plains, we are watching 'bucked' wildlife openings. These vital food sources consist of feed—cut-and-piled grain—layered high enough so that the birds can feed from the top of the buck to the bottom all winter long. This surpasses the benefit of food plots, which could be covered by as much as four feet of snow, so deep, in fact, that no birds could get to the feed."

"Moving farther south in the Great Plains, we have a program called Operation Big Sky, which plants shelter belts to provide winter protection and roosting areas."

Keck sees other improved management methods. "Radio telemetry will continue to help us understand expanded populations of birds." He offers the example of the reintroduction of the Gould's to Arizona, where the birds have gone into such rugged habitat that only radio telemetry can help track them.

He also sees more management by private landowners and management on private lands. "Some 96 percent of land in this country is under private ownership, so there has to be emphasis from nongovernmental organizations, as well as state wildlife agencies. More and more people are doing plantings, not only of wintering food, but also plantings that can help at that critical time when the poults hatch. Clovers and other legumes are great insect attractors. Programs like our Project Help will prescribe what private landowners, from small to big, can do to benefit wild turkeys, which, of course, benefits other game and nongame species."

Private landowners will figure into management in other ways. "Utility, coal and timber companies must partner on research and planting projects. Utilities, for example, spend tens of millions of dollars on herbicides or mowing just to maintain rights of way. Those companies can

Expanding our turkey hunting fraternity to women and children is key to the sport's future.

Hunter education will continue to improve, ushering in more knowledgeable, safety-conscious, better-prepared and responsible turkey hunters. They will join their friends and elders in continuing the wild turkey hunting tradition.

allow sportsmen, wildlife agencies and organizations like NWTF to plant and maintain wildlife openings in areas with powerlines and pipelines. It would enhance wildlife habitat and reduce the companies' maintenance costs. Programs for youths on these lands can allow children to become stewards of these resources."

The federal government can help too. "It can help facilitate across-the-border transfers, such as Gould's from Mexico to Arizona or Easterns from the U.S. to Canada, to better assure successful transplants," Keck explains, remembering delays that hurt the Gould's restoration effort.

He's hopeful of seeing more federal financial aid for matching funds from private conservation organizations, as well as legislation supportive of wild turkey management, which would eliminate some existing obstacles.

Beyond telemetry, technology will continue to play a part in turkey management in the 21st cen-

tury. "Some of the work done through satellite imagery will help us better inventory the various components of habitat. It will identify strengths and weaknesses and give us a quick rundown of where we need to focus more effort on improving habitat."

Keck sees other ways technology will affect the turkey hunter. Licensing will become easier, for example, when computer licensing is more widely available. Hunter education will improve also. "Computer simulators will make great strides beyond the 8- to 12-hour hunter education courses that continue in some states even today. There will be interactive video, where students will seemingly experience firsthand a variety of situations that they would be confronted with in the field. I think modern technology will help make more knowledgeable, responsible hunters."

The leader of the National Wild Turkey Federation, with good reason, has made the future of the wild turkey and turkey hunting seem bright. The road to the future does, however, also have its potholes, if not roadblocks.

"Habitat loss would have to be number one on the list. Urban sprawl causes the extensive loss of habitat to human encroachment on a daily basis. This has to be the greatest challenge we face in this country, not just with wild turkeys, but with all the wildlife that we enjoy."

Social trends and financial needs are related problems turkey hunters will face. "People have really lost touch with the land. Even though turkey hunting numbers are growing, hunting numbers in general are declining. If our numbers decrease, our political clout lessens, our agencies lose economic clout, and as a whole, we lose an awful lot in the way we're able to manage and educate and help pass on the legacy."

"We have to do everything possible to ensure that our state and federal resource agencies are well funded with long-term and continuous dollars. Hunters have paid the way for conservation in the past, and they will, to a large part, in the future. But we must broaden the dollar base from a wider array of outdoorsmen and women who use public land and depend on state and federal wildlife resource agencies to help fund their outdoor interests."

The National Wild Turkey Federation

Leader of the National Wild Turkey Federation (NWTF) since 1981, Rob Keck is the executive vice president and chief executive officer of the organization. During his tenure, the NWTF membership has grown from 25,000 to 180,000 members. The number of conservation projects funded has increased to more than 8,400, and the money spent for wildlife conservation has surpassed $90 million.

As Keck explains it, the mission of NWTF is twofold: first, to conserve the American wild turkey; second, to preserve the turkey hunting tradition. "'Conservation' is a pretty broad word. It would include all the different forms of research, management and education that we're involved with in working with this great game bird. And we make no bones about it that hunting is a very, very important part of conservation."

The organization's accomplishments are impressive. Keck lists some of them:

• **Assisting state wildlife agencies in restoring wild turkeys.** That has included dollars, human energy, the acquisition of the birds and the boxes used to transfer the birds. "Restoration and introduction of wild turkeys certainly have to rank up on top of the list," Keck remarks.

• **Educating the public to the logistics of turkey hunting.** "For the hunters who didn't have a father or grandfather who hunted turkeys and could pass along the important information, we fill a big need."

• **Creating a feeling of stewardship.** "Not only do we answer the people who ask what can they do—for instance, how can they improve habitat—but we help emphasize the value of these birds. In places where turkeys were being poached as quickly as they were being released, we helped to change public attitudes."

• **Funding wild turkey research.** "We've spent millions of dollars. It's been highlighted by the symposia we hold every five years. Better than 90 percent of the research done in this country on the wild turkey has been funded at least in part by the NWTF."

The organization's lifeblood is grass roots support—individual members and local chapters. Members receive an outstanding magazine, a handsome decal and a subscription to an informative tabloid.

For more information on the National Wild Turkey Federation, write P.O. Box 530, Edgefield, SC 29824-0530 or call (800) THE-NWTF.

TURKEY HUNTERS SHOPPING DIRECTORY

Turkey hunters have a multitude of choices when it comes to buying clothing, calls, guns and ammunition. It can be helpful to build up a library of catalogues, price lists and other literature. Here is a directory of manufacturers and outlets for those supplies.

AC	=	Accessories	**CA**	=	Calls	**F**	=	Firearms
AM	=	Ammunition	**CL**	=	Clothing	**FA**	=	Firearms Accessories
B	=	Boots	**D**	=	Decoys	**V**	=	Videotapes

Activ Industries, Inc.
1000 Zigor Rd.
Kearneysville, WV 25430
(304) 725-0451
AM

Adco Sales Inc.
10 Cedar St.
Woburn, MA 01801-6365
(617) 935-1799
FA

Aimpoint
7700 Leesburg Pike
Ste. 310 A
Falls Church, VA 22043
(703) 749-2320
FA

Aimtech Mount Systems
P.O. Box 223
Thomasville, GA 31799
(912) 226-4313
FA

API Outdoors, Inc.
P.O. Box 1432
Tallulah, LA 71282
(318) 574-4903
AC

Bass Pro Shops (Redhead)
2500 E. Kearney
Springfield, MO 65898
(417) 873-5082
AC, AM, F, FA, B, CA, CL, D, V

L. L. Bean
Freeport, ME 04033-0001
(800) 221-4221
AC, B, FA

Benelli
21480 Pacific Blvd.
Sterling, VA 20166
(703) 450-1900
F

Beretta U.S.A.
17601 Beretta Dr.
Accokeek, MD 20607
(301) 283-2191
F

Blount, Inc. (CCI, Speer)
P.O. Box 856
Lewiston, ID 83501
(800) 624-3640
AM

Blount, Inc. (Simmons, Weaver)
201 Plantation Oak Pkwy.
Thomasville, GA 31792
(912) 227-9053
FA

Briley Mfg., Inc.
1230 Lumpkin
Houston, TX 77043
(713) 932-6995
FA

Broner, Inc.
1750 Harmon Rd.
Auburn Hills, MI 48326
(800) 543-4482
CL

Browning
One Browning Place
Morgan, UT 84050
(801) 876-2711
B, CL, F, FA

Bushnell Sports Optics Worldwide
9200 Cody
Overland Park, KS 66214
(913) 752-3400
FA

Bushy Ridge Products
P.O. Box 897
Jackson, AL 36545
(334) 246-1791
AC

Butler Creek Corporation
290 Arden Dr.
Belgrade, MT 59714
(406) 388-1356
FA

C-More Systems
7553 Gary Rd.
Manassas, VA 20109
(703) 361-2663
FA

Cabela's Inc.
1 Cabela Dr.
Sidney, NE 69160
(308) 254-5505
AC, AM, F, FA, B, CA, CL, D, V

Carry-Lite, Inc.
5203 W. Clinton Ave.
Milwaukee, WI 53223
(414) 355-3520
D

Carter Canvas Company, Inc.
1710 Dutch Fork Rd.
Immo, SC 29063
(803) 781-2289
CL

Connecticut Valley Arms, Inc.
5988 Peachtree Corners East
Norcross, GA 30071
(800) 251-9412
F, FA

DeLorme Mapping Co.
2 DeLorme Drive
Yarmouth, ME 04096
(800) 452-5931
A (maps)

Dixie Gun Works, Inc.
P.O. Box 130
Union City, TN 38261
(901) 885-0561
F, FA

Dunham Bootmakers
P.O. Box 1289
Lewiston, ME 04243
(800) 843-2668
B

Duofold
7540 Wilson Dr.
2 Windsor Plaza, Ste. 205
Allentown, PA 18195
(800) 448-8240
CL

Federal Cartridge Company
900 Ehlen Dr.
Anoka, MN 55303
(612) 323-2300
AM

Field & Stream
P.O. Box 47366
Plymouth, MN 55447
(612) 557-8060
CL

Field & Stream Rugged Footwear
519 W. Laurel St. #2
San Diego, CA 92101
(619) 232-9884
B

Fieldline
1919 Vineburn Ave.
Los Angeles, CA 90032
(213) 226-0830
AC

Flambeau Products Corporation
15981 Valplast Rd.
Middlefield, OH 44062
(216) 632-1631
D

Flint River Outdoor Wear, Inc.
5731 B. Miller Ct.
Columbus, GA 31909
(706) 562-0005
CL

G&H Decoys, Inc.
P.O. Box 1208
Henryetta, OK 74437
(918) 652-3314
D

Grabber Performance Group
16550 Franklin Rd.
Fort Bragg, CA 95437
(707) 961-0776
AC

Grouse Hill Taxidermy
240 Unadilla Rd.
Putnam Valley, NY 10579
(914) 528-7178
A (taxidermy)

Haas Outdoors, Inc. (Mossy
  Oak)
200 E. Main St.
West Point, MS 39773
(800) 331-5624
AC, CL, V

Haydel's Game Calls, Inc.
5018 Hazel Jones Rd.
Bossier City, LA 71111
(318) 746-3586
CA

Higdon Motion Decoys
1 Universal Way
Metropolis, IL 62960
(618) 524-3385
D

Hogdon Powder Company
P.O. Box 2932
Shawnee Mission, KS 66201
(913) 362-9455
AM

Hornady Mfg. Company
P.O. Box 1848
Grand Island, NE 68802
(308) 382-1390
AM

Hunter's Specialties, Inc.
  (H.S. Strut)
6000 Huntington Ct. NE
Cedar Rapids, IA 52402-1268
(319) 395-0321
AC, CL, CA, V

Image Country Camouflage
  Company, Inc.
111B Corporate Park E.
La Grange, GA 30241-0058
(706) 883-6332
CL

Ithaca Gun Company, LLC
891 Rt. 34B
King Ferry, NY 13081
(315) 364-7182
F

Johnny Stewart Wildlife Calls
5100 Fort Ave.
Waco, TX 76714
(817) 772-3261
CA

Kicks Industries, Inc.
698 Magnolia Church Rd.
Statesboro, GA 30458
(912) 587-2779
CA

Knight & Hale Game Calls
488 Canton Blue Springs Rd.
Cadiz, KY 42211
(502) 924-1755
GC, V

Leupold & Stevens, Inc.
P.O. Box 688
Beaverton, OR 97075
(503) 646-9171
FA

Longbeard Industries, LLC
P.O. Box 127
Eutaw, AL 35462
(800) 897-8981
AC

M. L. Lynch Company, Inc.
500 W. Jefferson
Thomasville, GA 31792
(912) 226-5793
CA

Marlin Firearms Company
100 Kenna Dr.
North Haven, CT 06473
(203) 239-5621
F

Michael's of Oregon
  Company
P.O. Box 13010
Portland, OR 97213
(503) 255-6890
AC, FA

Modern Muzzleloading, Inc.
P.O. Box 130
Centerville, IA 52544
(515) 856-2626
A, F, FA

O.F. Mossberg & Sons, Inc.
7 Grasso Ave.
North Haven, CT 06473
(203) 230-5300
F

Mountain State
  Muzzleloading Supplies,
  Inc.
Box 154-1
Williamstown, WV 26187
(304) 375-7842
AC, F

National Wild Turkey
  Federation
P.O. Box 530
Edgefield, SC 29824
(800) THE-NWTF
AC, CA, CL, FA, V

Nikon, Inc.
1300 Walt Whitman Rd.
Melville, NY 11747
(516) 547-4200
FA

North Wind Decoy
  Company
1005 N. Tower Rd.
Fergus Falls, MN 56537
(218) 736-4378
D

Oak Country Camo
  Company, Inc.
2169 Greenville Rd.
LaGrange, GA 30241
(706) 883-6332
CL

Philip S. Olt Company, Inc.
P.O. Box 550
Pekin, IL 61555
(309) 348-3633
AC, CA

Outland Sports (Feather Flex
  Decoys, Lohman Game
  Calls, M.A.D. Game Calls)
4500 Doniphan Dr.
Neosho, MO 64850
(417) 451-4438
CA, D, FA, V

Outlaw Decoys
10907 E. Marietta
Spokane, WA 99206
(509) 927-2750
D

Pella Productions, Inc.
835 Broadway
Pella, IA 50219
(515) 628-3092
CL

Penn's Woods Products
P.O. Box 306
Delmont, PA 15626
(412) 468-8311
CA

Pentax Corp.
35 Inverness Dr. E.
Englewood, CO 80112
(303) 799-8000
FA

Perfection Turkey Calls, Inc.
P.O. Box 164
Stephenson, VA 22656
(703) 667-4608
CA

Peters Game Calls
P.O. Box 8158C
Lima, OH 45805
(419) 229-PETE
CA

Primos, Inc.
P.O. Box 12785
Jackson, MS 39236
(601) 366-1288
AC, CA, V

Quaker Boy, Inc.
5455 Webster Rd.
Orchard Park, NY 14127
(716) 662-3979
AC, CA, V

QuietWear by Reliable
P.O. Box 563
Milwaukee, WI 53201
(414) 272-5084
CL

Rattlers Brand
115 E. Main St.
Thomaston, GA 30286
(706) 647-7131
AC, CL

Realtree Outdoor
  Products, Inc.
P.O. Box 9638
Columbus, GA 31908
(706) 569-9101
V

Future of Turkey Hunting

Red Wing Shoe
314 Main St.
Red Wing, MN 55066
(651) 388-8211
B

Redfield, Inc.
5800 E. Jewell Ave.
Denver, CO 80224
(303) 757-6411
FA

Remington Arms Company
870 Remington Dr.
Madison, NC 27025
(800) 243-9700
AC, AM, F

Roy Rhodes Championship
  Calls
5700 Ferguson, Ste. 8
Bartlett, TN 38134
(901) 385-1115
CA, V

Rich-N-Tone Products
348 New Byhalia Rd.
Collierville, TN 38017
(901) 853-6430
AC, CA

Pete Rickard, Inc. (Scotch
  Game Calls)
P.O. Box 292
Cobleskill, NY 12043
(800) 282-5663
AC, CA

Rocky Shoes and Boots, Inc.
39 E. Canal St.
Nelsonville, OH 45764
(800) 421-5151
B

W.C. Russell Moccasin Co.
P.O. Box 309
Berlin, WI 54923-0309
(920) 361-2252
B

Skyline Camouflage Inc.
184 Ellicott Rd.
West Falls, NY 14170
(716) 655-0230
CL

Southern Game Calls
545 Oakhurst
Clarksdale, MS 38614
(601) 627-1967
CA

Spartan Outdoors
W-4228 Church St.
Hingham, WI 53031
(800) 666-2674
CL

Stoeger Industries
5 Mansard Ct.
Wayne, NJ 07470
(800) 631-0722
FA

Sturm, Ruger & Company, Inc.
200 Ruger Rd.
Prescott, AZ 86301
(520) 541-8824
F

Sure-Shot Game Calls, Inc.
P.O. Box 816
Groves, TX 77619
(409) 962-1636
CA

Tasco
2889 Commerce Pkwy.
Miramar, FL 33025
(954) 252-3649

10X Products Group
2915 LBJ Freeway
Ste. 133
Dallas, TX 75234
(972) 243-4016
CL

Texsport
P.O. Box 55326
Houston, TX 77255
(713) 464-5551
CL

Thompson/Center Arms
  Company
P.O. Box 5002
Rochester, NH 03867
(603) 332-2394
F

Timber Ghost Camouflage
10022 C.R. 3070
Rolla, MO 65401
(573) 341-2946
C

Traditions Performance
  Muzzleloading
P.O. Box 776
Old Saybrook, CT 06475
(860) 388-4656
F, FA

Trebark Camouflage
3434 Buck Mountain Rd.
Roanoke, VA 24014
(540) 774-9248
CL

Truglo, Inc.
4110 Shady Hill Dr.
Dallas, TX 75229
(214) 358-2810
FA

U.S. Repeating Arms, Inc.
275 Winchester Ave.
Morgan, UT 84050
(801) 876-3440
F

Walker's Game Ear, Inc.
P.O. Box 1069
Media, PA 19063
(800) 424-1069
AC

Walls Industries
P.O. Box 98
Cleburne, TX 76033
(800) 447-9327
CL

Weatherby Inc.
3100 El Camino Real
Atascadero, CA 93422
(805) 466-1767
F

WestArk Hunting Apparel
P.O. Box 4349
Ft. Smith, AR 72914
(800) 782-9007
CL

White Muzzleloading
  Systems
25 E. Hwy. 40
Roosevelt, UT 84066
(801) 772-5996
F, FA, V

Wilderness Sound
  Productions, Ltd.
4015 Main St. A
Springfield, OR 97478
(503) 741-0263
CA, V

Williams Gun Sight Company
7389 Lapeer Rd.
Davison, MI 48423
(810) 658-2140
FA

Winchester Ammunition
427 N. Shamrock St.
East Alton, IL 62024
(618) 258-2000
AM

Wing Supply
P.O. Box 367
Greenville, KY 42345
(800) 388-9464
AC, FA, B, CA, CL, D, V

Wolverine Footwear Group
9341 Courtland Dr.
Rockford, MI 49351
(616) 866-5000
B

Woods Wise Products
P.O. Box 681552
Franklin, TN 37068
(800) 735-8182
AC, CA, D, CL

Woolrich Inc.
1 Mill St.
Woolrich, PA 17779
(717) 769-6464
CL

Carl Zeiss Optical
Sports Optics Division
1015 Commerce
Petersburg, VA 23803
(800) 441-3005
FA

INDEX